Herb... ...ff Stranks

G. Ger... ...Lewis-Jones

MORE! 1

Student's Book

CAMBRIDGE
UNIVERSITY PRESS

HELBLING
LANGUAGES

	Grammar	Language Focus and Vocabulary	Skills	MORE!
STARTER SECTION	• subject pronouns • present simple of *be* • possessive adjectives • plural nouns	• classroom objects and language • greetings • saying hello • numbers • asking about age • international words • colours • days of the week **Sounds right** the alphabet	• listen to and understand international words • talk about favourite foods • listen to and complete a dialogue to introduce yourself • read about other people and where they are from • listen to and complete facts about other people • spelling • talk about myself and others **A Song 4 U** *Alphabet stars*	**Check your progress** Starter section
UNIT 1 Hello!	• present simple of *be* • questions with *Who* • possessive adjectives	• feelings **Sounds right** days of the week	• say hello / introduce yourself • ask how people feel • read and write about days of the week and feelings **A Song 4 U** *The Weekend is for me*	**Learn MORE through English** **Using the World Wide Web**
UNIT 2 In the classroom	• imperatives • questions with *Who, Where, Why, What, What colour?* • prepositions	• classroom objects **Sounds right** /ə/	• ask and say where things are • listen to and understand imperatives • write about your desk	**Check your progress** Units 1 and 2 **Learn MORE about culture** **The United Kingdom** **Read MORE for pleasure** **Sunday mornings**
UNIT 3 My bedroom	• *There is/are* • possessive *'s* • adjectives	• words for furniture • rooms in the house	• describe rooms and furniture • listen to information about a zoo • read a story • write about your ideal room	**Learn MORE through English** **Sleep**
UNIT 4 Who's that boy?	• *have got* • the indefinite article	• parts of the body • countries and nationalities **Sounds right** /h/	• talk about nationality • describe people • talk about possessions • listen to and understand physical descriptions • read descriptions of people • write a description of yourself or a friend	**Check your progress** Units 3 and 4 **Learn MORE about culture** **School in England** **Read MORE for pleasure** **The wide-mouthed frog**
UNIT 5 What's for lunch?	• present simple (positive) • spelling: third person singular • adverbs of frequency	• food **Sounds right** question intonation	• make and reply to offers and requests • talk about what you eat • read about different diets and foods • write about your eating habits	**Learn MORE through English** **Food from around the world**
UNIT 6 Time for change	• present simple (negatives, questions and short answers) • object pronouns	• daily activities	• ask and tell the time • talk about routines • read about other people's routines • write about your day **A Song 4 U** *The master of time*	**Check your progress** Units 5 and 6 **Learn MORE about culture** **Multicultural Britain** **Read MORE for pleasure** **The world's best detective**

	Grammar	Language Focus and Vocabulary	Skills	MORE!
UNIT 7 Shopping!	• demonstrative adjectives and pronouns • countable and uncountable nouns • *How much?/How many?* • *some/any*	• clothes **Sounds right** /ð/	• talk about prices • talk about clothes • listen to and understand a dialogue in a food shop • read and understand a story • describe someone in the class • write about clothes you like to wear	Learn **MORE** through English **Maths made easy**
UNIT 8 My family	• *can* for ability • *can* questions and short answers • *like/love/hate doing*	• family members	• talk about abilities • ask for permission • talk about things you like doing • talk about your family • read a text about a family • listen and understand what activities people do • write a poem **A Song 4 U** *Heaven*	**Check your progress** Units 7 and 8 Learn **MORE** about culture **School breakfast clubs** Read **MORE** for pleasure **Teenage web designer**
UNIT 9 What are you doing?	• present continuous (positive, negative, questions and short answers) • forming words with *-ing*	• telephone numbers • ordinal numbers • months of the year	• talk on the phone • talk about birthdays • listen to and identify sounds • read about birthdays in different cultures • write a postcard **A Song 4 U** *Mr Muddle is never right!*	Learn **MORE** through English **The Carnival of the Animals**
UNIT 10 Right now	• articles • present simple vs. present continuous	• computers • free-time activities **Sounds right** *the*	• make invitations • talk about your free-time • listen and talk about pets • read and understand a short article **A Song 4 U** *Super-sonic surfer*	**Check your progress** Units 9 and 10 Learn **MORE** about culture **Spend spend spend** Read **MORE** for pleasure **Poems**
UNIT 11 Where were you?	• past simple of *be* (positive, negative, questions and short answers) • past time expressions	• furniture **Sounds right** *was/were*	• ask and say where people were • say where things are • read, listen to and understand a mystery story • write about your day yesterday	Learn **MORE** through English **Money**
UNIT 12 Game over!	• past simple (positive)	• shops **Sounds right** /t/ /d/ /ɪd/	• say when you were somewhere • talk about shopping • read short articles and match them to the correct information • listen to a story and correct sentences **A Song 4 U** *A summer holiday*	**Check your progress** Units 11 and 12 Learn **MORE** about culture **Free-time activities** Read **MORE** for pleasure **Great Mysteries of the World: Flight 19**

Word list   page 140

STARTER SECTION

Vocabulary The classroom

1 Look at the picture. Write the number of the objects.

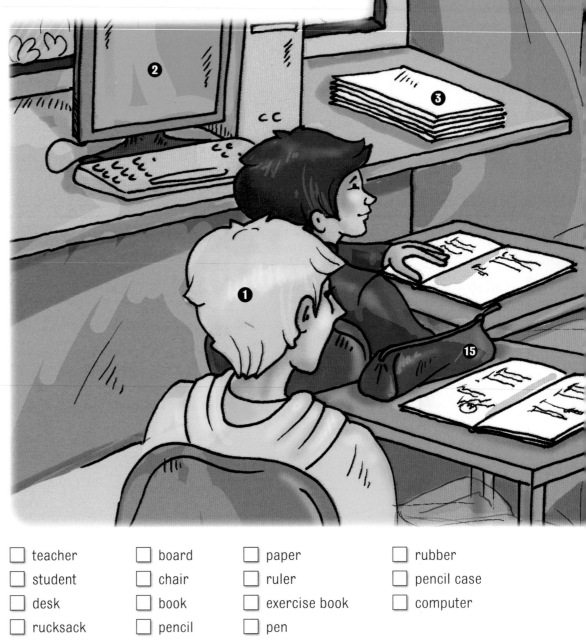

- ☐ teacher
- ☐ student
- ☐ desk
- ☐ rucksack
- ☐ board
- ☐ chair
- ☐ book
- ☐ pencil
- ☐ paper
- ☐ ruler
- ☐ exercise book
- ☐ pen
- ☐ rubber
- ☐ pencil case
- ☐ computer

2 Listen to the sentences. How do you say them in your language?

I don't understand.

Can you repeat that, please?

What's the homework, please?

Can you spell *pen*, please?

Listen to the CD.

Do exercise 3.

Look at the board.

Copy the sentences.

Get talking Greetings

 3 Match the greetings to the correct picture. Write the number. Then listen and write the expressions under the pictures.

- ☐ Good evening.
- ☐ Good morning, Mrs Jones.
- ☐ Goodbye, Mum.
- ☐ Good morning, Luke.
- ☐ Good afternoon, Mrs Jones.
- ☐ Good night, Luke.

- ☐ Good night, Mum.
- ☐ Good afternoon, Luke.
- ☐ Goodbye, Luke.
- ☐ Hi, Luke.
- ☐ Hello, Jenny.

1 ....

2 ....

3 ....

4 ....

5 ....

6 ....

7 ....

8 ....

9 ....

10 ....

11 ....

Get talking Saying hello

 4 **Listen and repeat the dialogues.**

Shireen	Hi, May. How are you?
May	Hello, Shireen. I'm fine. And you?
Shireen	Great, thanks.

Ahmed	Hello, Luke. How are you?
Luke	I'm fine. How are you, Ahmed?
Ahmed	I'm fine, thanks.

 5 **Listen and complete the dialogues.**

Dialogue 1

Helga	Hi, Jan. How [1]........... you?
Jan	Hello, Helga. [2]........... fine, thanks. And you?
Helga	Great, thanks.

Dialogue 2

Abi	Hi, José [3]........... are you?
José	I'm fine, thanks, Abi. And [4]...........?
Abi	I'm OK, thanks.

6 **Now practise the dialogues with a partner.**

Vocabulary Numbers

6 **1** **Listen and write the numbers.**

six
eight
seventeen
twelve
fifteen
~~two~~

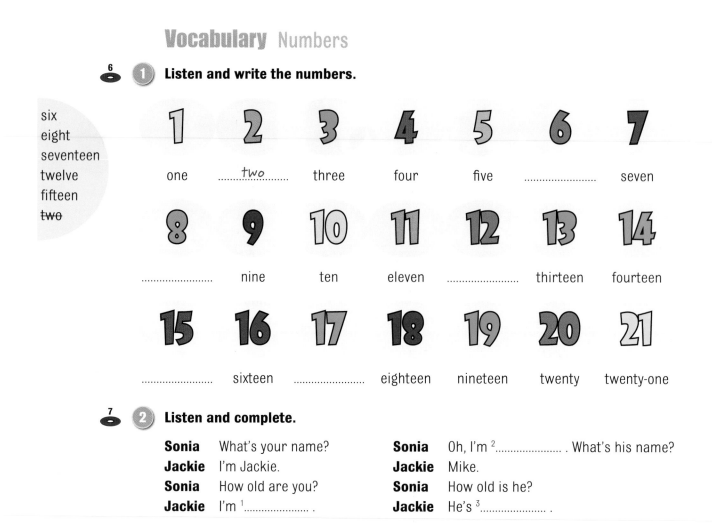

1	2	3	4	5	6	7
one	*two*	three	four	five	....	seven

8	9	10	11	12	13	14
....	nine	ten	eleven	....	thirteen	fourteen

15	16	17	18	19	20	21
....	sixteen	....	eighteen	nineteen	twenty	twenty-one

7 **2** **Listen and complete.**

Sonia What's your name?
Jackie I'm Jackie.
Sonia How old are you?
Jackie I'm ¹.................... .

Sonia Oh, I'm ².................... . What's his name?
Jackie Mike.
Sonia How old is he?
Jackie He's ³.................... .

Get talking Asking about age

3 **Look at the photos and the names and ages. Close your books and ask and answer with a partner.**

A How old is Mike?
B He's 12.
A That's right. / That's wrong – he's …

MIKE 12

JANE 17

SIMON 15

JACKIE 16

ERICA 11

TOM 14

Subject pronouns Singular

Liam	Hi! **I**'m Liam.
Mrs Wade	How old are **you** Liam?
Liam	**I**'m 10.
Mrs Wade	And your friends?
Liam	Kylie. **She**'s 11. Connor. **He**'s 10.
Mrs Wade	And your pet?
Liam	My tortoise? **It**'s 135!

1 **How do you say these words in your language?**

1 I ....
2 You ....
3 He ....
4 She ....
5 It ....

2 **Write the correct pronoun.**

1 ....._You_.....
2 ....
3 ....
4 ....
5 ....

Present simple of *be* Singular, positive

3 **Use the dialogue above to complete the table.**

I	**am**		I'[1]...........	
You	**are**		You'**re**	
He		10.	He[2]...........	10.
She	**is**		She[3]...........	
It			It[4]...........	

4 **Rewrite the sentences. Use the short form.**

1 I am Spanish. ....._I'm Spanish._..... 4 He is scared. ....
2 She is nice. .... 5 You are friendly. ....
3 It is late. ....

5 **Complete the sentences with the correct short form.**

1 Hello. I......
   Fergus.
2 It...... a dog.
3 Mark is my
   friend. He...... 13.
4 This is Nadia.
   She...... nice!
5 Hello, Tom!
   You...... late!

Possessive adjectives Singular

| My name's Nadia. | Her name's Bess | What's **its** job? |
| What's **your** name? | What's **his** name? | |

6 Use the grammar box above to complete the table.

Subject pronoun	I	you	he	she	it
Possessive adjective	¹ _my_	²	³	⁴	⁵ ....

7 Complete the sentences. Use *my*, *your*, *his* or *her*.

1 .... name's Wayne Rooney.

2 Hi! I'm Steve. What's .... name?

3 .... name's Jennifer Lopez.

4 .... name's José.

8 Circle the correct word.

1 Hi, *I / my* name is Kelvin.
2 *She / Her* is 15.
3 What's *you / your* name?
4 Dawn is *she / her* friend.
5 *He / His* is friendly.
6 *I / My* am scared.

9 Match the questions and the answers.

1 What's your name?
2 How old are you?
3 Who is your favourite teacher?
4 Who is your best friend?
5 How old is your best friend?

A I'm 10.
B My favourite teacher is Mr Glass.
C My name's Liz.
D My best friend is Cheri.
E She's 10.

10 Write your own answers to the questions in Exercise 9.
Then ask and answer with a partner.

Listening

 1 **Listen and write the numbers. Then write the correct word under the pictures.**

ice cream
hamburgers
hot dogs
apples
pizza

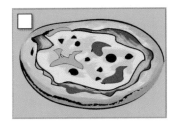

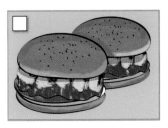

....

....

Speaking

 2 **Listen and repeat. Then practise other dialogues with a partner.**

What's your favourite food?

Apples.

Listening

3 **Listen to the interview and complete the dialogue.**

Interviewer	What's [1]..................... name?
Girl	Kirsty.
Interviewer	Where are [2]..................... from?
Girl	I'm from London.
Interviewer	How old [3]..................... you?
Girl	I'm thirteen.
Interviewer	What's [4]..................... favourite food?
Girl	Hamburgers.
Interviewer	What's [5]..................... favourite number?
Girl	[6]..................... seven.

Reading

  Read and complete.

Hi, my name's Michael and I'm from Manchester. I'm 14. My dog's name is Leo and my cat's name is Suzy. They're nice. My favourite food is fruit and my favourite number is 10.

Hello, I'm Anna and I come from Budapest, in Hungary. I'm 15 years old and 15 is my favourite number! My favourite food is chicken – it's great! My pets are Peter, my hamster, and Piri, my dog.

1   ...Michael... is 14.
2   .... is 15.
3   Michael is from ....
4   .... is from Hungary.

5   Michael's favourite .... is 10.
6   Anna's favourite food is ....
7   Leo is a ....
8   Peter is a ....

Listening

  Listen and complete the table.

	City	Age	Favourite food	Favourite number
Alice	York	12	pizza	17
Ben				
Karen				
Christopher				
Hannah				
Daniel				

A Song 4 U Alphabet Stars

12 **6** **Listen and sing.**

(yeah, we've got the Alphabet Stars
let's move ahead)

A, B, A, B, C, yo, A, B, C is easy for me,
D, yes, E and F, D, E, F is easy for Jeff!
G, H, G, H, I, yeah, come on, hey, le, le
let me try.
J, yes, K and L, J, K L, it's easy to spell.

Chorus (x 2)
We are the Alphabet Stars, yes
Alphabet Stars,
That's what we are.

M, N, M, N O, yo,
M, N O, let's go, let's go.
P, yes, Q and R,
P, Q, R, yes, you're a star.
S, T, S, T, U, it's easy, yes, it's easy for Sue.
Now, it's uh, now it's V,
V, that's so easy for me!

Chorus (x 4)

W, X and Y and Z,
That's the A, B, C.
Come on now, let's move ahead,
Come on, yo, let's move ahead,
Come on, come on, let's move ahead.
Yeah, come on, let's move ahead.

Sounds right The alphabet

13 **7** **Listen and repeat. Which four letters are missing?**

1 A H J K
2 B C D E P T V
3 F L M N S X
4 Q U W
5 I Y

Get talking Spelling

14 **8** **Listen and repeat the dialogue. Then work with a partner and practise
dialogues with other names.**

International words

9 **Write the words under the pictures.**

taxi
pizza
bus
supermarket
football
hamburger
hotel
tennis

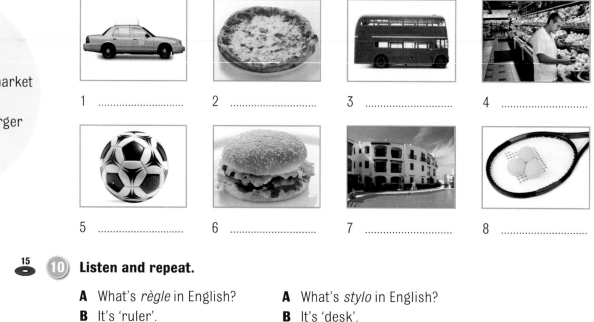

1 ....

2 ....

3 ....

4 ....

5 ....

6 ....

7 ....

8 ....

15

10 **Listen and repeat.**

A What's *règle* in English?
B It's 'ruler'.
A Yes, that's right.

A What's *stylo* in English?
B It's 'desk'.
A No, that's wrong.

11 **Work with a partner. Ask and answer questions about these objects. Use the dialogue from Exercise 10.**

Vocabulary Colours

16 **12** **Listen and write the numbers.**

☐ red ☐ green ☐ blue ☐ yellow ☐ black

☐ pink ☐ orange ☐ brown ☐ grey ☐ white

Vocabulary Days of the week

17 **13** **Put the days of the week in order. Write 1–7. Then listen and check.**

☐ Wednesday   **1** Monday

☐ Sunday   ☐ Tuesday   ☐ Friday

☐ Saturday   ☐ Thursday

Get talking Saying the days of the week and colours

14 **Work with a partner. Ask and answer.**

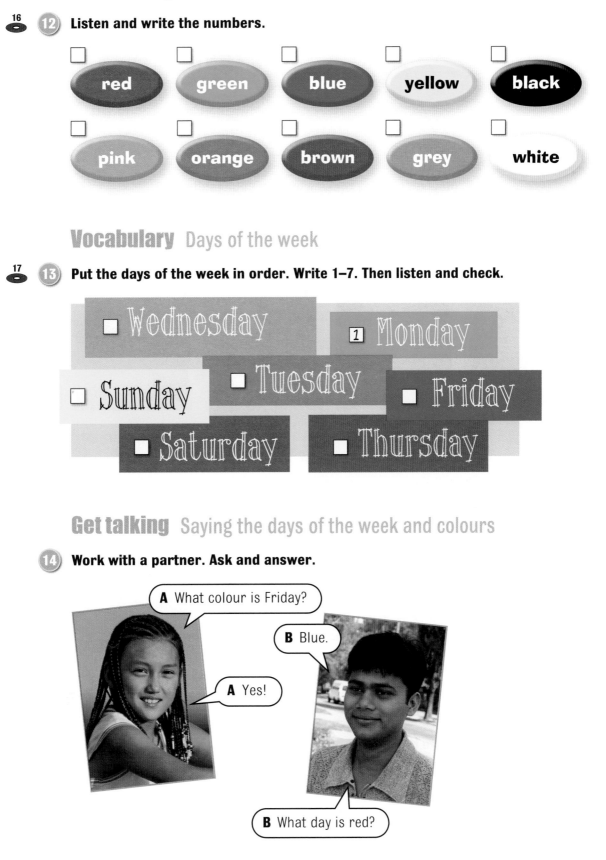

A What colour is Friday?

B Blue.

A Yes!

B What day is red?

Subject pronouns Plural and singular

We're from Brazil.

You're from Argentina – right?

They're from Italy.

1 **How do you say these words in your language?**

1 We .... 2 You .... 3 They ....

2 **Write the correct subject pronoun.**

❶ You

❷ ....

❸ ....

❹ ....

❺ ....

Present simple of *be* Plural, positive

3 **Use the cartoon in Exercise 1 to complete the table.**

Full form			Short form	
We	**are**		We[1]...........	
You	**are**	friendly.	You[2]...........	friendly.
They	**are**		They[3]...........	

4 **Rewrite the sentences. Use the short form.**

1 They are lovely. *They're lovely.* 4 She is Greek. ....

2 You are my friend. .... 5 He is Steve. ....

3 We are from London. .... 6 I am from York. ....

5 **Write the correct short form: '*m*, '*re*, or '*s*.**

1 They......... from Cardiff.

2 We......... 12!

3 They......... my books.

4 I......... Italian.

5 He......... English.

Possessive adjectives Plural and singular

> **Sasha** Hi Jane! Hi Liam! Is this **your** dog?
> **Jane and Liam** Yes, it's **our** dog?
> **Sasha** And is that **your** cat?
>
> **Jane and Liam** No, it's **their** cat.
> **Dorota and Steffi** Yes, it's **our** cat.

6 Use the dialogue above to complete the table.

Subject pronoun	we	you	they
Possessive adjective	¹.............	² *your*	³.............

7 Write *our, my, their, your, his* or *her* under the pictures.

1 Are they ....
  hot dogs?

2 She's Maria. ....
  house is nice!

3 They're Vladimir and Lek.
  And that's .... dog!

4 This is .... house.

5 I'm Marta and she's
  Alice. She's .... friend!

6 What's .... name?

Plural nouns

8 Look at the box and complete the rule.

Singular	Plural
He is my friend.	They are my friend**s**.
Bess is a dog.	Bess and Baron are dog**s**.

* To make nouns plural, add ¹............

* Some plurals are irregular:

one child	two **children**	one woman	two **women**
one man	two **men**	one person	two **people**

9 Make the sentences plural.

1 The house is nice.
  The houses are nice. ....

2 The man is English.
  ....

3 Your horse is lovely.
  ....

4 My friend is from London.
  ....

Get talking Talking about myself and others

18 **10** **Listen and tick the sentences the people say.**

1
- ☐ I'm Rebecca.
- ☐ I'm Veronica.
- ☐ I'm from Oxford.
- ☐ I'm from Cambridge.
- ☐ I'm 11.
- ☐ I'm 12.
- ☐ I'm in Year 7.
- ☐ I'm in Year 8.

2
- ☐ I'm Robert.
- ☐ I'm Roger.
- ☐ I'm from York.
- ☐ I'm from Cork.
- ☐ I'm 12.
- ☐ I'm 13.
- ☐ I'm in Year 7.
- ☐ I'm in Year 8.

3
- ☐ We're Sam and Catherine.
- ☐ We're Karen and Benny.
- ☐ We're from London.
- ☐ We're from Liverpool.
- ☐ We're 13.
- ☐ We're 14.
- ☐ We're in Year 8.
- ☐ We're in Year 9.

4
- ☐ We're Helen and Michael.
- ☐ We're Hannah and Bill.
- ☐ We're from Oxford.
- ☐ We're from York.
- ☐ We're 12.
- ☐ We're 13.
- ☐ We're in Year 8.
- ☐ We're in Year 9.

11 **Talk about the boys and girls from Exercise 10.**

1 Veronica's from .... She's ....
   She's in ....
2 .... from .... He's ....
   He's in ....
3 .... and .... 're from ....
   They're .... They're in ....
4 .... and .... 're from ....
   They're .... They're in ....

12 **Talk about yourself.**

I'm ....
I'm from ....
I'm ....
I'm in ....

Check your progress Starter Section

1 Complete the classroom words.

1 t _ _ _ _ _ r
2 d _ _ k
3 r _ l _ r
4 p _ n
5 r _ bb _ r
6 s _ _ _ _ _ t
7 p _ _ _ _ l c _ _ e
8 p _ _ _ r
9 b _ _ k
10 ch _ _ r

[10]

2 Match the words to the correct numbers.

1 fifteen   a 18
2 twenty-one   b 16
3 nineteen   c 15
4 eight   d 21
5 sixteen   e 19
6 eighteen   f 8

[6]

3 Complete the sentences with the correct short form of *be*.

1 She .... English.
2 They .... from Brazil.
3 We .... 20.
4 He .... friendly.
5 I .... from London.
6 You .... 13.

[6]

4 Complete the dialogue.

A ¹........................ afternoon, Mrs Carter.
B Hello, Tim. How ²........................ ³........................?
A ⁴........................ fine, thanks. And
   ⁵........................?
B Great ⁶........................ .

[6]

5 Circle the correct answer.

1 Her name's Rosa. *She / Her* is Brazilian.
2 This is my dog. It *is / are* friendly.
3 We *is / are* from Liverpool.
4 Rob and Dan are from Bath. *They / We* are in class 8A.
5 I love sport. *My / His* favourite sport is football.
6 We're English, but *our / your* favourite food is pizza!

[6]

6 Write the plural form of these words.

1 child   ....
2 man   ....
3 woman   ....
4 person   ....
5 house   ....
6 friend   ....

[6]

7 Complete the names of the days of the week.

1 S _ _ _ _ _ _ _
2 M _ _ _ _ _
3 F _ _ _ _ _
4 T _ _ _ _ _ _ _
5 S _ _ _ _ _
6 T _ _ _ _ _ _

[6]

8 Complete the sentences.

1 They're Emma and Sarah. That's .... house.
2 We're Paul and James. .... school is there.
3 You're from Argentina. Are they .... rucksacks?
4 They're English. That's .... car.

[4]

TOTAL [50]

My progress so far is ...

☺ brilliant!   ☐

😐 quite good.   ☐

☹ not great.   ☐

In this unit

You learn

- present simple of *be*
- questions with *Who*
- possessive adjectives
- words for feelings

and then you can

- say hello / introduce yourself
- ask how people feel

19

1 **Listen and read.**

Nadia	Hi, Steve.
Steve	Hello, Nadia. How are you?
Nadia	I'm fine, thanks. And you?
Steve	I'm OK. Oh, look! Dogs! I'm scared of dogs.
Nadia	What's his name?
Mrs Jones	Baron. He's friendly.
Nadia	And what's his name?

Mrs Jones	She's a girl. Her name's Bess.
Nadia	Hello, Bess. Oh, you're a nice dog!
Mrs Jones	And what's your name?
Nadia	Oh, sorry! My name's Nadia, and this is Steve.
Mrs Jones	Hello, Steve. Hello, Nadia. I'm Mrs Jones. I'm new here.
Steve	Nice to meet you, Mrs Jones.

2 **Write the names under the pictures.**

~~Bess~~
Baron
Mrs Jones
Steve
Nadia

① Bess
②
③
④
⑤

3 **Write the names in the spaces.**

1 .... is fine.
2 .... is scared of dogs.
3 .... is friendly.
4 .... is a nice dog.
5 .... is new here.

Get talking Saying hello / introducing others

20 **4** **Listen and complete the dialogues.**

Dialogue 1

Olivia Hello, Emma. How are you?
Emma Hi, Olivia. I'm fine, thanks. How [1]............. you?
Olivia Great, thanks.
Emma Olivia, this [2]............. Lucas. Lucas, this [3]............. Olivia.
Lucas Hi, Olivia. Nice to meet you.
Olivia Hi, Lucas. Nice to meet you too.

Dialogue 2

Noah Hi, Anna. Meet Michael and Tony. They [4]............. new here.
Michael Hi, Anna.
Anna Hi, Michael.
Tony Hello, Anna. How [5]............. you?
Anna Hi, Tony. I'm fine, thanks. And [6].............?
Michael I'm OK, thank you.
Anna Oh, sorry. I [7]............. late. Bye!
Michael and Tony Bye, Anna.
Noah Bye, bye!

5 **Act out dialogues in class. Use your own names.**

Language Focus

Vocabulary Feelings

1 Follow the lines and ask and answer questions.

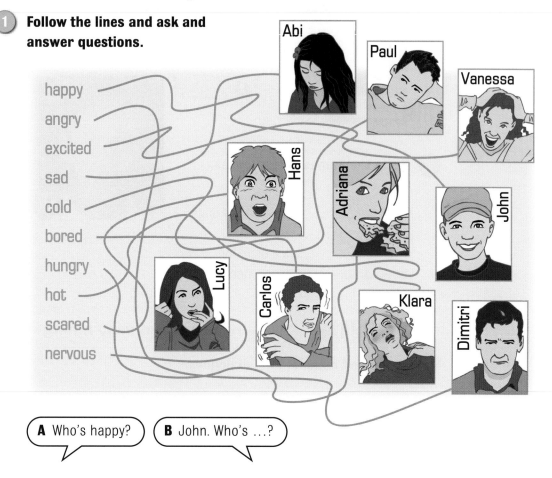

happy
angry
excited
sad
cold
bored
hungry
hot
scared
nervous

Abi · Paul · Vanessa · Hans · Adriana · John · Lucy · Carlos · Klara · Dimitri

A Who's happy?

B John. Who's …?

Get talking Asking how people feel

2 Work with a partner. Look at the pictures then close your books and ask and answer.

Victor · Maria · Sally and Liz · Pedro · Kendra

A What's wrong with Victor?

B He's tired. What's wrong with Sally and Liz?

A They're scared.

Grammar

Present simple of *be* Positive

> **I'm** scared of dogs.
> **He's** (**She's** / **It's**) OK.
> **We're** (**You're** / **They're**) fine.
>
> I'm = I am
>
> He's / She's / It's = He is / She is / It is
>
> We're / You're / They're = We are / You are / They are

1 Complete the sentences with *'m*, *'re* or *'s*.

1 This is Katie. She............ from London.
2 I............ Victoria, not Vicky.
3 We............ scared of dogs.
4 Sandra and Zoe, you............ late!
5 Meet Brandon and Morgan. They............ new here.
6 Thank you, Jane. You............ great!
7 It............ a nice dog!
8 Isabel, meet Dominic. He............ my friend.

Present simple of *be* Negative

> **I'm not** from London.
> **You/We/They aren't** new here.
> **He/She/It isn't** OK.

2 Rewrite the sentences. Use the short form.

1 It is not cold. _It isn't cold._
2 We are not English.
   ....
3 You are not late.
   ....
4 I am not angry.
   ....
5 She is not happy.
   ....
6 They are not friendly.
   ....

3 Complete the sentences. Use the short form.

1 It .... _isn't_ .... a dog. It's a cat!
2 They .... English. They're Italian.
3 He .... angry. He's hungry.
4 You .... right. You're wrong.
5 She .... Mrs Jones. She's Nadia!
6 We .... thirteen. We're fourteen.
7 It .... my dog. It's his dog.
8 I .... Steve. I'm Mike.

Present simple of *be* Questions and short answers

> **Am I** scared of dogs?
> Yes, **you are.** / No, **you aren't.**
>
> **Are you OK?**
> Yes, **I am.** / No, **I'm not.**
>
> **Is he/she/it** friendly?
> Yes, **he/she/it is.** / No, **he/she/it isn't.**
>
> **Are we/you/they** new here?
> Yes, **we/you/they are.** / No, **we/you/they aren't**.

4 Complete the questions and short answers.

1 ...._Is_.... Nadia Italian?   No, she ..._isn't_.. .
2 .... you bored?   Yes, I ....
3 .... I right?   No, you ....
4 .... it a cat?   Yes, it ....
5 .... they excited?   Yes, ...
6 .... we wrong?   No, ...
7 .... Steve sixteen?   No, ...
8 .... you hot?   No, ...

Questions with *Who...?*

A **Who's** he?
B Pierre. He's from Paris.

A **Who are** they?
B Mario and Maria. They're from Madrid.

How do you say *Who...?* in your language?

5 **Write the questions.**

1 *Who's she* ....?
    She's Mrs Jones.
2 ....?
    He's my friend, Steve.
3 ....?
    They're Steve and Nadia.
4 ....?
    I'm Sarah Jones.
5 ....?
    We're Mike and Jenny Smith.
6 ....?
    She's the new teacher.
7 ....?
    Coldplay – they're my favourite band.
8 ....?
    He's our friend Tony.

Possessive adjectives Revision

I'm Peter. This is **my** friend Tom.
Lily, is this **your** dog?
This is my friend. **His** name's Mike.
Meet Nadia and **her** friend Steve.
It's a nice dog. What's **its** name?
We're happy. **Our** favourite band's in town!
Girls and boys, I'm **your** new English teacher.
Meet Jane and James and **their** friends from France.

6 **Listen and repeat the rap.**

21

This isn't my cat.

It isn't your cat.
Oh, no!

It isn't his cat.

It's her cat.

Yes, I'm her cat.
Meow!

This isn't our dog.

It isn't your dog.

Of course not. It's their dog.

That's right, I'm their dog.

Woof, woof!

Reading

1 Read the story.

MAX IS HAPPY

❶ Max is in his car. His car's beautiful – and fast. He's happy – he's very happy!

❷ Tom's his friend. He's in the car, too. He isn't happy. He's nervous – he's very, very nervous!

❸ Mr and Mrs Cross are at the bus stop. They aren't happy. They're cold – they're very, very cold!

❹ Mrs Bing is in front of her shop. She isn't happy. She's angry – she's very, very angry!

❺ The duck's in the road. It isn't happy. It's scared – it's very, very scared!

❻ Max isn't in his car now, and he isn't very happy. But the duck's happy and Mrs Bing is happy. And Mr and Mrs Cross are happy. And Tom's happy, too. They're all happy – they're all very, very happy!

2 Complete the table.

	In Picture	In Picture
Max	1: *is very happy*	6: *isn't very happy*
Tom	2:	6:
Mr and Mrs Cross	3:	6:
Mrs Bing	4:	6:
the duck	5:	6:

3 Work with a partner. Draw an expression on the faces then ask and answer.

Tim

Fred and Lucas

A Is Ella happy?
B No, she isn't.
She's sad.
Is Maria happy?
A Yes, she is.

Maria

Ella

Sounds right Days of the week

22 **4** **Listen and repeat.**

Monday, Tuesday, Wednesday – sad!
Thursday, Friday – they aren't bad!
Saturday and Sunday – great!
Tomorrow's Monday – don't be late!

Reading

5 **Read the sentences and write the day of the week above the picture.**

1 Monday

2

3

4

5

6

7

It's Monday morning.
Sue's tired.

It's Tuesday evening.
Sue's bored.

It's Wednesday afternoon.
Sue's angry.

It's Thursday morning.
Sue's nervous.

It's Friday afternoon.
Sue's excited. Tomorrow's
the weekend.

It's Saturday afternoon.
Sue's busy. She's shopping.

It's Sunday. Sue's happy.

A song 4 U The weekend is for me

6 Listen and complete, then sing.

excited (x 2) nervous (x 2)
bored (x 2) angry (x 2)
tired (x 2)

On Monday I'm so [1]..........,
as [2].......... as I can be.
I really don't like Monday,
no, Monday's not for me.
(*No, it's not, not for me.*)

On Tuesday I'm so [3].........., yeah,
as [4].......... as I can be.
There's nothing good on TV,
no, Tuesday's not for me.
(*No, it's not, not for me.*)

Chorus
It's just another day,
another day, you see.
It's a day like many others,
it's just not good, not good
for me.

On Wednesday I'm so [5]..........,
as [6].......... as I can be.
I've got a lot of homework,
no, Wednesday's not for me.
(*No, it's not, not for me.*)

On Thursday I'm so [7]..........,
as [8].......... as I can be.
We have a test on Thursday,
no, Thursday's not for me.
(*No, it's not, not for me.*)
Chorus

On Friday I'm [9]..........,
as [10].......... as I can be.
Tomorrow is the weekend,
the weekend is for me.

The weekend's here,
the weekend's here, you see.
The weekend is fantastic,
it's just the best for me!
The weekend is fantastic.
The weekend is for me! (x 2)

Writing for your Portfolio

7 How do you feel during the week? Write a short description.

On Monday I'm not tired. I'm excited...

Information Technology

Key words

World Wide Web (WWW)
internet research
web page
search engine
search for

type
select
click on
webquest
download

FACT FILE

- There are billions of pages on the Web. At present English is the main language on the Web.

- Google and Yahoo are two very popular search engines.

- To search for pictures only, go to www.google.com and click on *images*.

Web Images Groups News Froogle^New! more »
SEARCH
Google Search | I'm Feeling Lucky
Search: ⊙ the web ○ pages from the UK

Then type a word, e.g. *London*. A second later you have lots of beautiful pictures.

- When you use Google, these tricks help you find information.

You type:	You find:
London people	pages with 'London' and 'people'
London OR Paris	pages with 'London' or 'Paris'
London –people	pages with 'London', but not with 'people'
concerts in London	pages with the exact phrase 'concerts in London'

1 **Read the facts about the *More!* website.**

This is what you find on www.cambridge.org/elt/more

- Fun stories to read
- Interesting interviews and other texts to listen to
- Interactive grammar and vocabulary exercises

It is easy to find your way round the *More!* website.

- Go to www.cambridge.org/elt/more
- Click on extra resources
- Click on a unit
- Select the activity you want to do

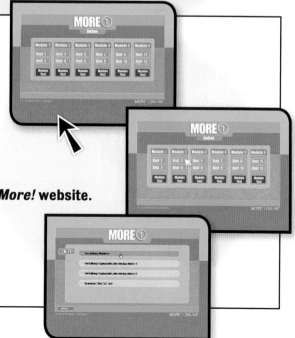

2 The *More!* Webquest. Go to the *More!* website and write the answers to these questions.

1 How many activities are there on the More! website for Unit 10?
2 There is a story in Unit 10 called Mrs Bing's pet shop. What is a 'snark'?
3 In Unit 6 there is a listening called The Pirates Parade. Who is Toby's pet?

4 Which unit has a grammar exercise on time?
5 In Unit 12, what is the Get Talking activity about? Do the activity then practise the dialogues with a partner.

Mini-project

3 Work in groups. Use the Web.

1 Find the names of three big cities in England.
2 Choose one of these cities. Find three pictures of it. Download the pictures.
3 Find out how many people live in the cities.
4 Find the name of a hotel there. Find a picture of it.
5 Find the name of a museum or a school there.
6 Find the name of a football club.

4 Write a report. Include your pictures.

File   Edit   View   Window   Tools   Help

Report: Our internet research

Our three big cities in England are London, Manchester and Liverpool.

The city of our choice: Manchester

Number of people: 400 000

Name of a hotel: The Palace Hotel

Football club: Manchester United

Here are some more pictures of Manchester:

The Palace Hotel

The football stadium

The Manchester Museum

A big shopping street

In this unit

You learn
- imperatives
- questions with *Who, Where, Why, What, What colour?*
- words for classroom objects
- prepositions

and then you can
- ask and say where things are

24 ① Listen and read.

Kate Nadia, don't sit there. Sit here, next to me.

Nadia OK, Kate. Thanks. What's the matter, Steve?

Steve Where's my pen?

Nadia I don't know. What colour is it? Red?

Steve No, it's black.

Kate Look! It's there, on the floor under the desk. Pick it up.

Nadia Who's she?

Kate I don't know – a new teacher, perhaps?

Miss Young Good morning. I'm Miss Young, your new teacher.

Nadia Good morning, Miss. You're right, Kate!

Steve Good morning, Miss.

Miss Young Why are you under the desk?

Steve My pen's on the floor, Miss. Ouch!

Miss Young Don't laugh – it isn't funny!

Kate Sorry, Miss.

Miss Young Well, come out and stand up. Who are you?

Steve Steve, Steve Johnson.

Miss Young Alright, sit down and be quiet. Right, everyone, open your books.

2 **Circle the correct answer.**

1 Nadia sits next to *Steve / Kate* .
2 Steve's pen is *black / red* .
3 His pen's on the *floor / desk* .
4 Miss Young is a new *pupil / teacher* .
5 Miss Young is *happy / angry* when the girls laugh.
6 She tells *Steve / everyone* to open *his / their* books.

25

3 **Complete with *in, on, under, next to, in front of* and *behind*. Then listen and check.**

1 It's .... the car.   2 It's .... the car.   3 It's .... the car.

4 It's .... the car.   5 It's .... the car.   6 It's .... the car.

Get talking Saying where things are

4 **Ask and answer questions about the animals and the cars.**

A Where's the red car?   **A** Where's the white cat?
B It's behind the …   **B** It's …

Language Focus

Vocabulary Classroom objects

26 **1** **Listen. Are the sentences you hear correct?**

Yes!

No, it's ....

2 board
10 overhead projector
9 window
4 door
1 CD player
5 desk
3 computer
8 chair
7 English book
6 floor

2 **Work with a partner. Cover the picture in Exercise 1. Ask and answer about the colour of the objects.**

A What colour's the desk?

B It's brown.

Get talking Saying where things are

3 **Draw the objects on the left in the picture. Work with a partner and ask and answer questions.**

ruler
rucksack
dictionary
pencil case
pen
rubber

A Where's the ...?

B Is it in/on/under/in front of/next to/behind the ...?

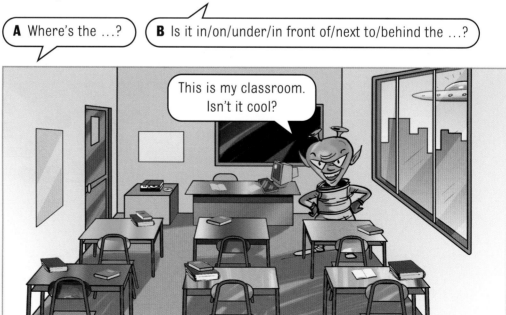

This is my classroom. Isn't it cool?

Grammar

Imperatives

 1 **Look at the dialogue on page 30 and complete.**

Open your books.
Don't sit there.
1 .... up.
2 .... it up.
3 .... down.
4 .... laugh.

2 **Write the phrases from the Grammar box under the correct picture.**

1 _Stand up_..............   2 ....

3 ....   4 ....

5 ....   6 ....

3 **Complete the sentences. Use the verbs below.**

| open | don't open | look | don't look |
| sit | don't sit | ~~be~~ | don't be |

1 ...._Be_.... quiet!   2 ....

3 .... down, please.   4 .... it!

5 .... sad.   6 .... there!

7 .... it!   8 ....

Questions with *Who, Where, Why, What, What colour?*

4 **Look at the dialogue on page 30 and complete.**

How do you say these question words in your language?

...................'s my pen?
.... colour is it?
...................'s she?
.... are you under the desk?

5 **Match the questions and answers.**

1 Where's Nadia?
2 What's his name?
3 What colour's your cat?
4 Who's Miss Young?
5 Why are you happy?

a She's the new teacher.
b Because my friend is here.
c She's in the classroom.
d It's black and white.
e It's Steve.

6 **Complete the questions.**

1 *What colour's* your bicycle?
   It's green.
2 .... her name?
   Sandra.
3 .... she?
   She's my new friend.
4 .... your dogs?
   They're in the house.
5 .... your favourite food?
   It's pizza.
6 .... your favourite film star?
   Matt Damon.
7 .... your schoolbag?
   Green and blue.
8 .... she sad?
   Because her friends aren't here.

7 **Reorder the words and write questions.**

1 from / where / you / are
   Where are you from ....?
2 is / what / favourite / band / your
   ....?
3 colour / are / dogs / what / his
   ....?
4 house / in / who / is / the
   ....?
5 Nadia / angry / is / why
   ....?
6 is / school / where / your
   ....?
7 their / what / car / colour / is
   ....?
8 teacher / favourite / who / your / is
   ....?

8 **Ask and answer questions with a partner. Use the question words to help you.**

...'s your house?
...'s your best friend?
...'s your favourite colour?
... are you from?
... your favourite band?
... your phone number?

In Green Street.

Skills

Listening

27 **1** **Complete the sentences then listen and check.**

walk   run   look
wait   open   see
put   put

1 .... your books in your bag.   2 .... in your pencil case.   3 .... to the bus stop.

4 .... for the school bus.   5 .... at your watch. It's 8 o'clock.   6 .... to school.

7 .... the door of your classroom.   8 .... the classroom is empty.   9 Oh, no! It's Saturday.

Sounds right /ə/

28 **2** **a Listen and repeat.**

1 tea<u>cher</u>   2 comp<u>uter</u>   3 play<u>er</u>   4 <u>under</u>   5 numb<u>er</u>   6 col<u>our</u>

29 **b Listen and repeat.**

1 Why is the teacher under the desk?
2 What colour is the teacher's computer?

Speaking

3 Work with a partner. Student A hides an object. Student B guesses where it is.

A Where's my pen?
B Is it in your rucksack?
A No, it isn't.
B Is it in your dictionary?
A No, it isn't.
B Is it under your pencil case?
A Yes, it is.

Writing for your Portfolio

4 Read Nadia's text about her messy desk. Write a similar text.

My desk is really messy! My pen is in my dictionary. My pencil case is on my rucksack, and my pencils are on the rucksack, too. My English book is behind the computer. My ruler is in my English book. My cat is on the computer. Where is my red pen? No idea!

MORE fun with Fido

Check your progress Units 1 and 2

1 **Write the classroom objects.**

1 w _ _ _ _ _   4 CD _ _ _ _ _ _
2 r _ _ _ _   5 d _ _ _
3 b _ _ _ _   6 c _ _ _ _   ☐ 6

2 **Complete the questions.**

1 .... you bored?
2 .... your pen on your desk?
3 .... Robbie Williams from London?
4 .... Sue and John happy?
5 .... your mother Italian?
6 .... the Maths test tomorrow?   ☐ 6

3 **Match the answers to the questions from Exercise 2.**

a .... No, she's from Poland.
b .... Yes, I am.
c .... No, he isn't.
d .... No, it's on Tuesday.
e .... Yes, it is.
f .... Yes, they are.   ☐ 6

4 **Reorder the dialogue.**

.... I'm nervous.
.... Hi, Lucy. How are you?
.... Because tomorrow is the Maths test.
.... Why not? What's the matter?
.... I'm not very happy.
.... Why are you nervous?   ☐ 6

5 **Complete the questions and answers.**

1 .... colour is your English book?

....

2 .... is your favourite actor?

....

3 .... is your house?

....

4 .... is your Maths teacher?

....

5 .... is the capital of England?

....   ☐ 10

6 **Write sentences in the negative form.**

1 I'm English.

....

2 They are hungry.

....

3 It's very hot today.

....

4 My teachers are friendly.

....

5 Hamburgers are my favourite food.

....

6 We're from Liverpool.

☐ 6

7 **Complete the sentences with the correct possessive adjective.**

1 That is Sarah. This is .... dog.
2 Hi, we're David and Tom. This is ....
   house.
3 They are students. That's .... school.
4 Hi, Tom! Is that .... dog?
5 **A** We're from France.
   B What are .... names?   ☐ 5

8 **Translate these phrases into your own language.**

1 Don't sit there.   ....
2 Open the window.   ....
3 Don't be sad.   ....
4 Look there.   ....
5 Don't be angry.   ....

☐ 5

TOTAL ☐ 50

My progress so far is …

☺ brilliant!   ☐
_____

😐 quite good.   ☐
_____

☹ not great.   ☐
_____

The United Kingdom

1 Match the descriptions to the correct picture then write the name of the city.

1 Hi, my name's Emma. I'm from .... It is the capital city of Scotland. My favourite place is the castle.

2 Hi, my name's Jake. I'm from ...., a Roman city in the north of England. There is a famous cathedral here.

3 Hello, I'm Melissa. I'm from .... in the south of England, near the sea. My favourite place here is the pier.

4 Hello, I'm David. I'm from ...., the capital of Wales. My favourite place is the rugby stadium. Rugby is a popular sport in Wales.

FACT FILE

COUNTRIES
England, Scotland, Wales and Northern Ireland

LANGUAGES
English, Welsh, Gaelic and Irish

POPULATION
59, 247, 000

ⓐ Brighton

ⓑ Cardiff

ⓒ York

ⓓ Edinburgh

30

2 Listen and complete the table.

	ENGLAND	SCOTLAND	WALES	N. IRELAND
Mountains		1	Snowdon	
Rivers	The Thames	The Tweed		2 ....
Lakes	Windermere	3		
Cities	London	Glasgow	4	5 ....

Belfast
The Bann
Ben Nevis
Loch Ness
Swansea

3 **Over 2 U!** Write a short description of the place where you live.

MORE! And now you can watch *Kids in the UK!* 📀

Learn MORE about culture

Sunday mornings

For **MORE!** Go to www.cambridge.org/elt/more and do a quiz on this text.

In this unit

You learn
- *There is/are*
- possessive *'s*
- words for furniture
- adjectives
- rooms in the house

and then you can
- describe rooms and furniture

31

1 Listen and read.

Nadia	What's your new bedroom like, Kate?
Kate	It's not very big. But it's really nice!
Steve	Are there any good posters?
Kate	Yes, a *Coldplay* poster and …
Jack	*Coldplay*? Who are they?
Steve	Oh, come on, Jack! They're really famous!
Kate	And there's a nice big wardrobe too.
Jack	Is there a bookshelf?
Kate	Yes, there is. It's next to the bed. It's small, but there aren't a lot of books in my room!
Nadia	Is there a light for reading in bed?
Kate	No, there isn't.
Steve	What else is there?
Kate	Well – there are blue curtains, two blue chairs and a desk. On the desk there's a …
Jack	Computer?
Kate	Yes, and there's a DVD player in it!
Nadia	Great! Can we watch some DVDs at your place?
Kate	Sure. Let's get Steve's *Coldplay* DVDs!
Steve	OK!

2 Reread the dialogue and answer Yes or No to the questions.

1 Is Kate's new bedroom big? ...No.
2 Are *Coldplay* famous? ....
3 Is Kate's bookshelf big? ....
4 Are her curtains green? ....

5 Is there a *Coldplay* poster in her room? ....
6 Is there a wardrobe in her room? ....
7 Are there a lot of books in her room? ....
8 Is there a DVD player in her computer? ....

Get talking Describing things

3 Find the opposites.

4 Look at the pictures. Ask and answer questions with a partner.

A Is the house big?   **B** No, it's very small.

big?   good?   friendly?

new?   early?

Language Focus

Vocabulary Furniture

32 **1** **Listen and write the numbers.**

- [ ] bed
- [ ] sofa
- [ ] stereo
- [ ] washbasin
- [ ] bath
- [ ] cooker
- [ ] fridge
- [ ] wardrobe
- [ ] desk
- [ ] armchair
- [ ] cupboard
- [ ] table
- [ ] TV
- [ ] curtains

2 **Look at the house then close your books and say what is in each room.**

In the living room, there's a television, and ....

In the kitchen, there are two chairs ....

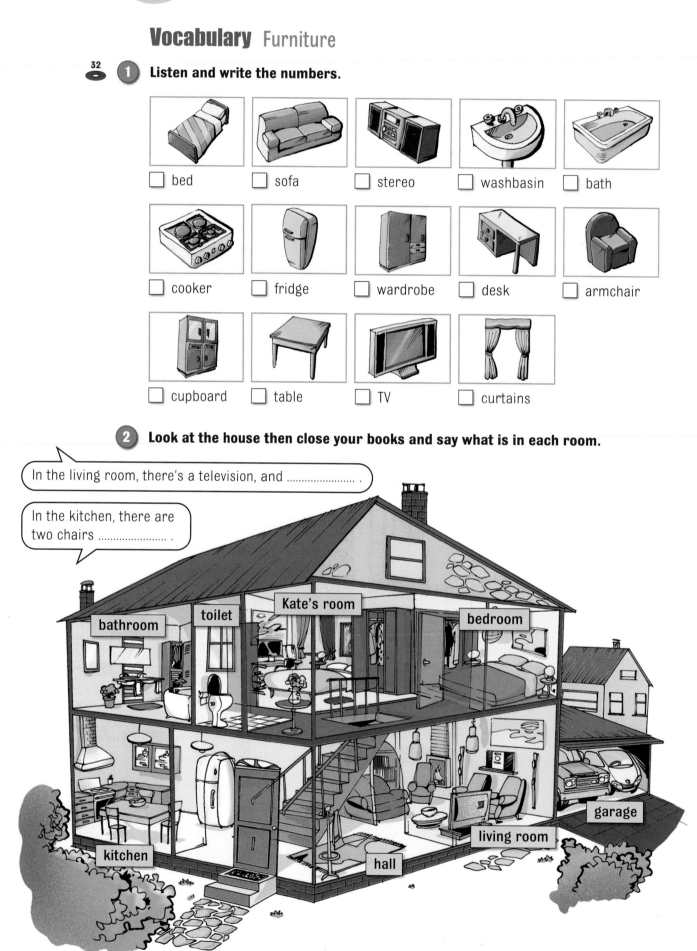

Grammar

There is/are

1   **Look at the dialogue on page 40 and complete the table.**

Positive	Negative	Questions	Positive	Negative
¹................... a nice big wardrobe.	There isn't a wardrobe.	³................... a bookshelf?	Yes, ⁵...................	No, there isn't.
²................... blue curtains.	There aren't curtains.	⁴................... any good posters?	Yes, there are.	No, there aren't.

2   **Complete the sentences with *There's* or *There are*.**

1 ....*There's*.... a desk in my room.
2 .... green curtains in his room.
3 .... a ham sandwich on the table.
4 .... a book on the floor.
5 .... six children in the room.
6 .... nice posters in our classroom.
7 .... a cat on my bed!
8 .... twenty-two children in my class.

3   **Complete with the correct form of *there is* or *there are*.**

1 ....*Is there*.... a TV in your room?
   No, ...
2 .... a car in the garage?
   Yes, ...
3 .... two beds in your room?
   No, ...
4 .... a sofa in your living room?
   No, ...
5 .... a lot of books in your bedroom?
   Yes, ...
6 .... a hall in your house?
   Yes, ...
7 .... a lot of sandwiches in the kitchen?
   No, ...
8 .... twenty-two desks in your classroom?
   Yes, ...

Get talking   Describing rooms and furniture

4   **Listen. Which rooms are the people in?**

 33

Conversation 1 ....
Conversation 2 ....
Conversation 3 ....
Conversation 4 ....

5   **Read the description of Nadia's ideal room.**

In my ideal room, there's a big bed and there are yellow curtains. Yellow is my favourite colour. There are lots of posters of pop stars and horses. There's a nice desk. On the desk, there's a computer with a big screen. There are two chairs and there are lots of shelves for my books and CDs. There is also a good stereo.

6 This is Steve's picture of Nadia's ideal room. There are three more errors. Find them.

Number 1: the bed is small.

Possessive 's'

Bob**'s** dog. (This is Bob. This is his dog.)

Nigella**'s** pizza. (This is Nigella. This is her pizza.)

7 Read the sentences and tick the correct column. Is the *s* a possessive or the short form of *is*?

	Possessive	is
1 Where are Steve's DVDs?	☐	☐
2 He's in the house.	☐	☐
3 They're Nadia's things.	☐	☐
4 Who's she?	☐	☐
5 The teacher's new.	☐	☐
6 Where are the teacher's books?	☐	☐

8 Rewrite the sentences. Replace the possessive adjectives with a name.

1 It's her desk. (Kate)
   It's Kate's desk.
   ....

2 They're his books. (Steve)
   ....

3 It's her room. (Nadia)
   ....

4 Where's his pen? (Jack)
   ....

5 Pizza is her favourite food. (Sally)
   ....

6 What is his favourite colour? (Steve)
   ....

Skills

Listening

1 Listen to the advert for the zoo. Number the sentences in the correct order.

Come to **Brighton Zoo!**

☐ **1** There's a great **café!**

☐ There are **pelicans** from California!

☐ There's a new pool for the **hippos.** It's great!

☐ There are **pony rides.** They're fantastic.

☐ There's a **playground** for the kids.

☐ There's a **pets corner** with rabbits and hamsters.

Adults: £12   Children under 10 free on Saturday

Do the quiz and send it in!

Yes   No

There are pelicans from California.

There's a café.

There's a swimming pool for kids.

There are hippo rides.

There's a pets corner with camels.

Children under 10 are free on Saturday.

Reading

The Lake District National Park, in the north-west of England, is very big. There are more than 2,000 square kilometres of hills, forests, green valleys and beautiful lakes. There are also lots of hotels, bed and breakfasts and campsites.

Daisy, Harriet, Dean, and Tom are on a school trip in the Lake District. They are at a campsite.

Tom	Help!
Dean	What's the matter?
Tom	There's a monster in the forest. A monster with six eyes.
Dean	What?
Tom	There's a monster with six eyes.
Dean	I'm tired. Tell Daisy.

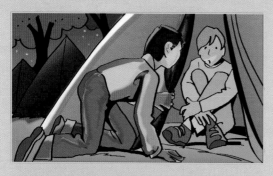

Tom	Daisy! Daisy!
Daisy	What's the matter?
Tom	There's a monster in the forest. A monster with six eyes.
Daisy	What?
Tom	There's a monster with six eyes.
Daisy	Tom, please. I'm tired. Tell Harriet.

Tom	Harriet! Harriet!
Harriet	What's the matter?
Tom	There's a monster in the forest. A monster with six eyes.
Harriet	What?
Tom	There's a monster with six eyes in the forest.
Harriet	OK, OK. Where's my torch?

Harriet	Where?
Tom	Over there! A monster with six eyes.
Harriet	Ah.
Tom	What is it?
Harriet	That's the monster! It's lovely. Three little owls in a tree.

3 **Who says what?**

It's lovely.

There's a monster with six eyes!

I'm tired. Tell Harriet.

1 .... 2 .... 3 ....

Speaking

4 **Work with a partner. Complete the dialogue with the phrases below then repeat it.**

What else is there?   Is there a bookshelf?
No, there isn't.   What's your new bedroom like, Kate?

Nadia   1 ....

Kate   Well, it's not very big.

Jack   2 ....

Kate   Yes, there is. It's small, but that's OK.

Nadia   Is there a light for reading in bed?

Kate   3 ....

Steve   4 ....

Kate   Well, there are blue curtains and two blue chairs. There's a desk, and on it there's a computer.

Writing for your Portfolio

5 **Describe your ideal room.**

In my ideal room there is ....
There are ....

Sleep

What is sleep? Sleep is the body's natural 'pause button'. During sleep, the muscles relax. Breathing gets slow. The heartbeat gets slow. The brain works differently too.

Why do we sleep? Scientists aren't sure. But they are sure that sleep is very important for the brain and the body.

The different stages of sleep – Human (35-year-old)

1 **Read the text. Write the stages of sleep in the correct place on the graph.**

Humans sleep in cycles of about 90–120 minutes. There are two types of sleep: non-REM (four stages) and REM sleep.

Stage one
During this stage of sleep, you are not really asleep. The body slows, the muscles relax. It is easy to wake up from this type of sleep.

Stage two
After ten minutes of light sleep, you start 'true sleep'. This lasts about 20 minutes. People breathe more slowly, the heart beats more slowly. Most sleep in the night is 'true sleep'.

Stage three
Breathing and heartbeat are very slow now.

REM sleep
REM means 'rapid eye movement'. This is because the eyes move very quickly.

The first rapid eye movement (REM) phase starts about 70 to 90 minutes after a person falls asleep. People have between three and five REM phases a night. They are not awake but the brain is awake and active. People dream during REM sleep but the body cannot move. That stops people 'acting' their dreams.

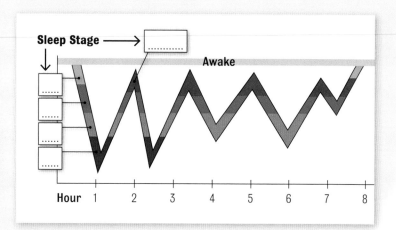

Stage four
Breathing is rhythmic. There is some muscle activity. It is difficult to wake up from this sleep.

FACT FILE

- You sleep about 8–10 hours.
- Human babies sleep about 16 hours a day.
- Old people sleep only 5–6 hours a night.
- Some animals sleep during the day. They are active during the night.
- Other animals (like the hedgehog) 'hibernate' – they sleep for 3–4 months during the winter.

2 **Answer the questions.**

1 How many non-REM stages of sleep are there?
2 When is the heartbeat at its slowest?
3 How many sleep cycles do people have each night?
4 What part of the body moves when a person dreams?

How animals sleep

Most animals sleep in cycles of non-REM and REM sleep. But not all animals sleep the same number of hours. What is important for animals is how safe they are when they are asleep. If an animal is in danger (for example, if other animals hunt it to eat) then it will sleep fewer hours.

3 **Read the texts below and match them to the correct photo. Write the correct letter in each photo.**

a   Leopards often sleep in trees. There they are safe from lions.

b   Bats sleep for nearly 20 hours a day. Nearly four hours is REM sleep.

c   Giraffes sleep about 4.5 hours a day. They have about 30 minutes of REM sleep a night.

d   Lions sleep about 13.5 hours a day. They only get up to drink. They hunt during the night.

e   Dolphins sleep for 10 hours a day, but only half of their brain is asleep. About 15 minutes is REM sleep.

Mini-project

4 **Keep a sleep diary for a week. Make a note of:**

- what time you go to bed
- what time you wake up
- if you dream
- how many times you wake up during the night
- if you sleep during the day (a siesta)
- how many hours you sleep a day in total

5 **After a week, compare your sleep diaries in class.**

4 Who's that boy?

In this unit

You learn
- *have got*
- the article *a/an*
- parts of the body
- countries and nationalities

and then you can
- talk about nationality
- describe people
- talk about possessions

35

1 Listen and read.

Kate	I've got some news.
Nadia	Oh? What?
Kate	There's a new boy in my brother's class!
Nadia	Oh really?
Kate	Yeah, he's French, I think. Or Spanish, perhaps – I'm not sure. His name's Alain.
Nadia	Alain? Well, he's probably French. It's a French name. Is he good-looking?
Kate	Yeah – he's tall, and he's got fair hair and blue eyes. And he's 14.
Nadia	Nice! Has he got an accent?

Kate	Yes, he has. It's great. I think foreign accents are really cool!
Nadia	Me too! Oh look! Is that him?
Kate	Yes, it is – and he's with Jennifer Parks!
Nadia	Never mind, Kate. Let's go to *Jerry's* for an ice cream. They've got great ice cream there!
Kate	Yeah, good idea. But I haven't got any money!
Nadia	That's OK, Kate. The ice creams are on me!

2 **Correct the wrong information in each sentence.**

1 There's a new girl in Kate's brother's class. ....boy..........
2 The boy's name is André. ....
3 He's got green eyes. ....
4 He's short. ....
5 Alain is 15. ....
6 Kate is happy that Alain's with Jennifer Parks. ....

Vocabulary Countries and nationalities

3 **Write the name of the country and the nationality in the correct place.**

Italy / Italian
France / French
~~England / English~~
Finland / Finnish
Germany / German
Spain / Spanish
Greece / Greek
Poland / Polish

Helsinki	
London	*England / English*
Berlin	
Warsaw	
Paris	
Madrid	
Rome	
Athens	

 4 **Listen and check.**

5 **Listen and repeat.**

❶ **Brazil** Brazilian **❷** **China** Chinese **❸** **Britain** British **❹** **The USA** American **❺** **Japan** Japanese **❻** **Austria** Austrian **❼** **Ireland** Irish **❽** **Turkey** Turkish

Get talking Talking about nationality

 6 **Ask and answer with a partner.**

A Where's she from?
B She's from Brazil.

A Oh, she's Brazilian.
B That's right.

Language Focus

Vocabulary Parts of the body

38 **1** Listen and write the numbers next to the words.

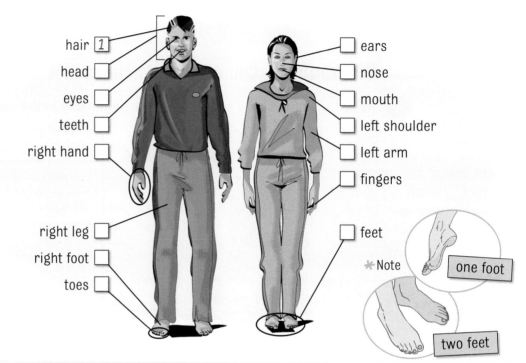

hair [1]
head ☐
eyes ☐
teeth ☐
right hand ☐

right leg ☐
right foot ☐
toes ☐

ears ☐
nose ☐
mouth ☐
left shoulder ☐
left arm ☐
fingers ☐

feet ☐

✳Note

one foot

two feet

Sounds right /h/

39 **2a** Listen and repeat.

1 hand   2 happy   3 head   4 hungry   5 hair   6 her

40 **2b** 1 Put your hands on your head.
2 Is he happy or hungry?

Get talking Describing people

3 Work with a partner. Describe one of the pictures below and ask your partner which one it is.

A He's got short hair, blue eyes, and a big nose.

B It's number three.

A That's right.

Grammar

have got

1 **Look at the examples from the dialogue on page 50. Complete the table.**

He**'s got** fair hair.
They**'ve got** great ice cream there!

I **haven't got** any money.
Has he **got** an accent? Yes, he **has**.

Positive			
I/you/we/they	**have** / '[1]............	got	long hair.
He/she/it	**has** / '[2]............		big eyes.

Negative			
I/you/we/they	**have not** / [3]............	got	long hair.
He/she/it	**has not** / **hasn't**		big feet.

Questions			Short answers	
			Positive	Negative
Have I/you/we/they	[4]............	long hair?	Yes, I/you/we/they **have**.	No, I/you/we/they **haven't**.
[5]............ he/she/it		big eyes?	Yes, he/she/it [6]............	No, he/she/it **hasn't**.

2 **Complete with *'ve* or *'s*.**

1 They.*'ve*..... got three cats.
2 He............ got a small nose.
3 She............ got green eyes.
4 I............ got long hair.
5 We............ got a big dog.
6 You............ got a nice accent.

3 **Complete with the correct form of *have got*. Use the short form.**

1 My friend.*'s*........ ...*got*.... three dogs.
2 I............ .... some news.
3 You............ .... nice hair.
4 My dog............ .... long ears.
5 They............ .... good ice cream in that place.
6 She............ .... a new DVD player.
7 He............ .... a French accent.
8 My brother and I............ .... green eyes.

4 **Write sentences using the negative form.**

1 He's got a dog. *He hasn't got a dog.*...........
2 I've got long hair.
....
3 Mum's got a new car.
....
4 We've got a big house.
....
5 You've got an accent.
....
6 The cat's got blue eyes.
....

5 **Reorder the words and write questions.**

1 cat / got / a / have / you
Have you got a cat.........................?
2 computer / got / she / has / a
....?
3 eyes / he / brown / got / has
....?
4 they / black / got / hair / have
....?
5 we / got / a / have / teacher / new
....?

6 **Write short answers.**

1 Has he got a cat?
Yes, he has. .... It's black and white.

2 Has she got black hair?
.... It's brown.

3 Have they got an accent?
.... – and it's very nice!

4 Have you got a new teacher?
.... – she's great!

5 Have we got ice cream in the fridge?
.... but we've got yoghurt.

Get talking Talking about possessions

7 **Listen and complete.**

41

1 **A** Have you got [1]............................. in your room?
B Yes, I have.
A What [2]............................. are they?
B They're [3]............................. .

2 **A** Have you got a [1].............................?
B Yes, I have.
A How [2]............................. is she?
B She's [3]............................. She's got
[4]............................. eyes and long hair.
A What's her [5].............................?
B Joanna.

3 **A** Have you got a [1].............................?
B Yes, we have.
A What's its [2].............................?
B Blackie.
A What [3]............................. is it?
B [4]............................., of course.
A How [5]............................. is it?
B Um – [6]............................., I think.

8 **Work with a partner. Ask and answer about people, animals and things.**

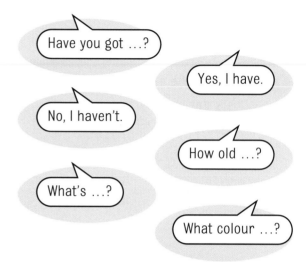

The indefinite article

9 **Look at the examples and complete the rule.**

a	book	an	apple
a	car	an	eye
a	house	an	ice cream
a	pen	an	orange
a	room	an	umbrella

✳ Before a noun that starts with a consonant use [1]...........

✳ Before a noun that starts with a vowel use [2]...........

10 **Complete with _a_ or _an_.**

1 I've got .....a..... banana and an apple.

2 Look! It's .... black cat!

3 There's .... armchair in my bedroom.

4 There's .... great ice cream place in town.

Skills

Listening

42

1 Listen and write the correct name in the box.

Linda
Alice
Barbara
Tom
Frank
Chris

❶

❷

❸

❹

❺

❻

Reading

2 Read the texts and match them to the correct picture.

❶

❷

❸

Madeleine is 12 years old. She's British. She's from London. She's got long, brown hair. Her eyes are blue.

Sara is 14 years old. She's German. She's from Berlin. She's got long, fair hair and blue eyes.

Sylvie is 13 years old. She's American. She's from Chicago. She's got short, brown hair and blue eyes.

Speaking

3 Look at the photos of teenagers of various nationalities (Italian, English, German, French, Spanish and Finnish). Try and guess the nationality of each one.

A I think the girl in photo 5 is from Spain. Look – she's got black hair.

B I think so too.

A I think the boy in photo 2 is from Germany.

B I don't think so, I think he's from Finland.

Writing for your Portfolio

4 Read the text and describe yourself or your friend.

My penfriend's name is Alex. He's thirteen. He's Finnish. He's from Helsinki. He's got fair hair and blue eyes. His favourite colours are blue and white. The Finnish flag is blue and white.

MORE fun with Fido

Come here!

Now I've got you!

Where's the butterfly?

Check your progress Units 3 and 4

1 **In which rooms can you find these things?**

1 cooker, fridge ....
2 wardrobe, bed ....
3 armchair, TV ....
4 washbasin, bath ....
5 car, bicycle ....

[ ] 5

2 **Circle the correct answer.**

1 *There is / are* two English girls in my school.
2 *Is / Are there* a good film on tonight?
3 *There isn't / aren't* a zoo in my town.
4 *There is / are* a lot of chairs in the classroom.
5 *Is / Are there* blue curtains in your room?
6 *There isn't / aren't* a lot of people in the cinema.

[ ] 6

3 **Tick the correct sentences and correct the wrong ones.**

1 There are three black dogs in the park. [ ]
2 Rome is a city beautiful. [ ]
3 There is two good actors in the film. [ ]
4 Are there two new CDs in your bag? [ ]
5 There is six books under my desk. [ ]

[ ] 5

4 **Write P if the *s* is possessive or A if it is an abbreviation of *is*.**

1 John's dogs are very friendly. ....
2 Where's your school? ....
3 Alison's not very happy today. ....
4 My mother's in her bedroom. ....
5 Susie's schoolbag is green and blue. ....
6 My cat's under the car. ....

[ ] 6

5 **Complete with the correct form of *have got*.**

1 My brother .... a new skateboard.
2 I .... Maths homework tonight.
3 .... you .... a big house?
4 She .... long, brown hair.

5 They .... two sisters.
6 My teacher .... a new motorbike.

[ ] 6

6 **Complete the table.**

Country	Nationality
1	Irish
France	4 ....
2	German
Japan	5 ....
3	Finnish
Poland	6 ....

[ ] 6

7 **Write the names for parts of the body.**

1 ysee ....
2 gnfire ....
3 thoum ....
4 hetet ....
5 drehsluo ....
6 sote ....

[ ] 6

8 **Answer the questions.**

1 Have you got a bicycle?
....
2 What colour hair have you got?
....
3 Has your teacher got a Brazilian accent?
....
4 Have your parents got a Japanese car?
....
5 What colour eyes have you got?
....

[ ] 10

TOTAL [ ] 50

My progress so far is ...

😊 **brilliant!** [ ]

😐 **quite good.** [ ]

☹ **not great.** [ ]

School in England

1 **Read the information about Sarah and complete the sentences with colours.**

Hi, I'm Sarah. I'm twelve years old. I'm at secondary school in year 8. It's a comprehensive school in the south of England. This is my school uniform. I hate it.

The shirt is ....
The skirt is ....
The jumper is ....
The jacket is ....

FACT FILE

Age 5 to 16 years old (compulsory)
Primary School 5 to 11 years old
Secondary School 11 to 16 or 18 years old

EXAMS

Key Stage 1	7 years old
Key Stage 2	11 years old
Key Stage 3	14 years old
Key Stage 4 (G.C.S.E.)	16 years old
A Levels	18 years old

2 **Look at the symbols and say which subject they are.**

43 **3** **Listen and complete Sarah's timetable.**

Time	MONDAY	TUESDAY	WEDNESDAY	THURSDAY	FRIDAY
8.30	R E G I S T R A T I O N				
8.45	[1]............	French	[3]............	Chemistry	Biology
9.25	[2]............	English	[4]............	Chemistry	Biology
10.00	B R E A K T I M E				
10.30	German	History	Physics	Maths	English
11.15	Geography	French	Physics	French	German
12.00	History	Maths	English	English	
12.45	L U N C H T I M E				
1.45	English	P.E.	Geography	[5]............	History
2.30	Maths	P.E.	Music	[6]............	Art & Design
3.15	.I.C.T	P.E.	Music	[7]............	[8]............
4.00	H O M E T I M E				

4 **Over 2 U!** **Write your timetable in English in your notebook.**

MORE! And now you can watch *Kids in the UK!* (DVD)

The wide-mouthed frog

Hi. I'm a wide-mouthed frog!

Frog	Hi. How are you?
Gorilla	I'm fine, thanks. What's your name?
Frog	I'm Freddy. I'm a wide-mouthed frog, and my favourite food is flies. What's your name?
Gorilla	I'm Gordon. I'm a gorilla. My favourite food is bananas.
Frog	Well, nice to meet you! Bye, gorilla!
Gorilla	Bye, frog!

Frog	Hi. How are you?
Bear	I'm fine, thanks. What's your name?
Frog	I'm Freddy. I'm a wide-mouthed frog. My favourite food is flies. What's your name?
Bear	I'm Betty. I'm a bear. My favourite food is honey.
Frog	Well, nice to meet you! Bye, bear!
Bear	Bye, frog!

Frog	Hi. How are you?
Crocodile	I'm fine, thanks. What's your name?
Frog	I'm Freddy. I'm a wide-mouthed frog. My favourite food is flies. What's your name?
Crocodile	I'm Carl. I'm a crocodile. My favourite food is ... wide-mouthed frogs!
Frog	Oh no, oh no, oh no! Bye!

!!!

For **MORE!** Go to www.cambridge.org/elt/more and do a quiz on this text.

What's for lunch?

In this unit

You learn
- present simple
- adverbs of frequency
- words for food

and then you can
- make and reply to offers and requests

44 **1** **Listen and read.**

Nadia	Hello. Can I have chicken and chips, please?
Woman	Of course, dear. Would you like cabbage, too?
Nadia	Um. Yes, please!
Woman	OK. Here you are.
Nadia	Thanks.
Jack	Cabbage? You never eat cabbage!
Nadia	That isn't true. I eat cabbage every week. Well, almost every week.
Jack	I hate cabbage. My dad loves it. He eats it every Sunday.
Woman	And for you, dear?
Jack	Oh, sorry! Er, can I have fish, please? With potatoes.
Woman	Would you like tomatoes?
Jack	No thanks. Just potatoes. Oh, and a yoghurt too, please.
Woman	OK. Here you are.
Nadia	I hate yoghurt, but my mother loves it. She eats it every day. She always takes yoghurt to work with her. Weird!
Jack	Oh? I eat it about four times a week. It's good for you!

2 Circle T (True) or F (False) for the sentences below.

1 Nadia wants chicken and chips. T / F
2 Nadia never eats cabbage. T / F
3 Jack likes cabbage. T / F
4 Jack's father likes cabbage. T / F
5 Jack wants fish with tomatoes. T / F
6 Nadia hates yoghurt. T / F

3 Reread the photostory and complete the dialogue.

Nadia   Hello. Can I have chicken and chips, please?
Woman   Of course, dear. ¹.. cabbage, too?
Nadia   Um. Yes, ²..!
Woman   OK. ³.. .

Woman   ⁴.. tomatoes?
Jack   No, ⁵.. .

45 **4** Listen and circle the correct word or expression.

1 **A** banana / apple
  B Yes, please. / No, thanks.

2 **A** orange / apple
  B Yes, please. / No, thanks.

3 **A** sandwich / hamburger
  B Yes, please. / No, thanks.

4 **A** ice cream / yoghurt
  B Yes, please. / No, thanks.

Get talking Making and replying to polite offers

5 Work with a partner. Ask and answer using the pictures below.

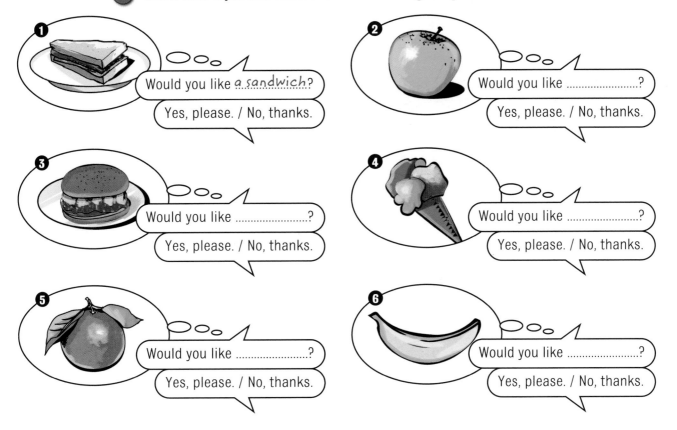

❶ Would you like *a sandwich*?
Yes, please. / No, thanks.

❷ Would you like ....?
Yes, please. / No, thanks.

❸ Would you like ....?
Yes, please. / No, thanks.

❹ Would you like ....?
Yes, please. / No, thanks.

❺ Would you like ....?
Yes, please. / No, thanks.

❻ Would you like ....?
Yes, please. / No, thanks.

Language Focus

Vocabulary Food

46 **1** **Listen and write the numbers.**

☐ onions	☐ tea
☐ egg	☐ rice
☐ bread	☐ fish
☐ cherries	☐ chicken
☐ oranges	☐ milk
☐ potatoes	☐ coffee
☐ sausages	☐ grapes
☐ spinach	☐ apples
☐ carrots	☐ orange juice

2 **Write the words from Exercise 1 under the correct category.**

Drinks   Vegetables   Fruit   Meat   Others

Sounds right Question intonation

3 **Listen and repeat.**

1 Can I have fish?
2 Would you like a sandwich?
3 Can I have an apple?
4 Would you like a banana?

Get talking Polite requests

4 **Work in pairs. Read the dialogue. Use the pictures to make different dialogues.**

Boy   Can I have chicken and rice, please?
Dinner lady Yes, of course. Here you are.

❶

❷

❸

❹

❺

❻

Grammar

Present simple Positive

 1 **Use the examples from the dialogue on page 60 to complete the table.**

I eat cabbage every week.
My dad loves it.
She eats it every day.

I/you/we/they	love	ice cream.
He/she/it	1	

2 **Put the words in the correct order to make sentences.**

1 watch / television / I / on Sunday .

....

2 homework / You / do / at home .

....

3 likes / My / spaghetti / mother .

....

4 fish / eat / on Fridays / We .

....

5 Shakira / to / He / listens .

....

6 on Monday / hate / school / They .

....

Spelling 3rd person singular

Notice the spellings.

Rela**x** – My dad always relax**es** after
Sunday breakfast.

Ki**ss** – She kiss**es** her mum goodbye.

Wa**sh** – He wash**es** his bike on
Saturdays.

Do – Mary do**es** the shopping.

Carr**y** – Steve carr**ies** the shopping for
his mum.

Watch – Jenny watch**es** DVDs every day.

3 **Complete the sentences with the correct form of the verb.**

1 My brother always .... (miss) the bus!

2 She .... (relax) at the weekend.

3 She .... (wash) her clothes on Saturdays.

4 Mike .... (watch) the football on Sundays.

5 My mother .... (tidy) the house all the time.

6 Jenny .... (do) her homework in the evening.

4 **Complete the sentences with the correct form of the verb.**

1 I ...*love*... (love) chicken sandwiches.

2 Steve .... (like) ice cream.

3 My brother and I .... (hate) football.

4 Her mother .... (take) her to school every day.

5 My father .... (teach) French at our school.

6 Sarah .... (go) to the cinema on Saturdays.

7 You .... (relax) at the weekend.

8 They .... (eat) chicken on Sunday.

5 **Complete the sentences with the words below.**

takes	eat	go	watches
goes	watch	take	eats

1 I .... DVDs on my computer.

2 We .... to school on Saturday mornings.

3 Kevin .... an apple after lunch.

4 Jack .... a bus to the football stadium.

5 I .... my brother to school.

6 My sister .... TV every day.

7 They .... a lot of fish.

8 Hal .... to the shopping centre on Saturday mornings.

Adverbs of frequency

 6 Read the examples and complete the rule.

I **often** play football.
I am **never** late.

✱ Frequency adverbs usually go
¹........................ the main verb.

✱ But they go ²........................ the verb *be*.

100%	I always	
↑	I usually	eat popcorn
	I often	at the
↓	I sometimes	cinema.
0%	I never	

7 Translate the words into your own language.

100%	**always**	....
	usually	....
	often	....
	sometimes	....
0%	**never**	....

8 Reorder the words and write sentences.

1 never / is / my father / late
   My father is never late.

2 is / Nadia / usually / hungry
   ....

3 often / am / nervous / I
   ....

4 goes / she / to the cinema / often
   ....

5 watches / sometimes / Jo / football on TV
   ....

6 usually / eat / breakfast / I / at home
   ....

9 Put the adverb in the correct place.

1 I watch TV on Sunday. (always)

2 My brother does his homework. (never)

3 James and Sally are hungry. (usually)

4 Our teacher is angry with us. (always)

5 Nadia and Kate go to the cinema together. (sometimes)

6 You are late. (often)

Tom never washes his dog!

10 Listen and complete the sentences.

48

sometimes	drink	always
eat	often	have	never

1 I .... tea for breakfast.
2 I .... soup for lunch.
3 I .... milk.
4 I .... an egg for breakfast.
5 We .... fish on Friday.
6 I .... rice and curry.

11 Talk about your favourite food.

I love chicken soup.
I never eat onions.

I hate bananas.
I often eat sausages.

Skills

Get talking Talking about what we eat

1 Read and tick the correct answer.

What do you eat?

1 I eat hamburgers or hot dogs

- ☐ every day.
- ☐ three times a week.
- ☐ once a week.
- ☐ once a month.
- ☐ I never eat hamburgers or hot dogs.

2 I eat vegetables

- ☐ every day.
- ☐ three times a week.
- ☐ once a week.
- ☐ once a month.
- ☐ I never eat vegetables.

3 I eat fruit

- ☐ every day.
- ☐ three times a week.
- ☐ once a week.
- ☐ once a month.
- ☐ I never eat fruit.

4 I eat chocolate, ice cream or sweets

- ☐ every day.
- ☐ three times a week.
- ☐ once a week.
- ☐ once a month.
- ☐ I never eat sweets.

2 Work in groups of 6–8 and talk about what you eat then tell the class.

> Two people in our group eat hamburgers or hot dogs three times a week.

Reading

 Read the texts.

http://www.kids

Kids around the world

| home | school | games | food | family |

I'm Li. I live in Shanghai, in China. In my family we often eat rice and noodles. I like noodles. We never eat cheese and we never drink milk. We often eat vegetables, such as cabbage, spinach and carrots and we sometimes eat fish. My father and my mother like fish, but I never eat fish. I hate it. I like fruit. My favourites are grapes, strawberries and oranges.

I'm Sunil. I live in Delhi, in India. Our family often has curry for lunch. We always have rice or bread with our curries. And we often drink yoghurt drinks. My sister hates yoghurt. She never has yoghurt drinks. She likes fruit and usually drinks mango juice. We always eat together at the same time.

Hi, I'm Jennifer. I live on Fraser Island, Australia. In our family, we often eat fish for dinner. My dad loves fishing. And we always have fruit: apples, bananas, kiwis, oranges, grapes and mangoes. I love mangoes. We never eat beef or pork. My mum and dad never buy it. We sometimes have curries. I love chicken curry.

 Circle T (True) or F (False) for the sentences below.

1 Li's family often eats rice and noodles. T / F
2 Sunil's sister hates yoghurt drinks. T / F
3 In Jennifer's family, they sometimes eat fish. T / F
4 In Li's family, they sometimes eat vegetables. T / F
5 Sunil's family often has rice or bread with curry. T / F
6 Jennifer likes mangoes very much. T / F

Listening

3 Complete the dialogue with the words on the left.

new
haven't
Thank you
Can I have a
there is no
fast food

Teacher	¹.. hamburger, please?
Dinner lady	Sorry, no hamburgers.
Teacher	OK. Can I have a hot dog, then?
Dinner lady	Sorry, we ². .... got hot dogs.
Jack	*(to Nadia)* Is he ³...?
Nadia	Yes, he is.
Jack	Sorry, Sir, ⁴.. junk food here.
Nadia	But there's a ⁵... place round the corner.
Teacher	Hmm. ⁶.. . Bye!
Jack	Sir? Can I come with you, Sir?

 4 Listen and check.

Writing for your Portfolio

5 Read the text and describe your eating habits.

I always have tea for breakfast. I sometimes have an egg. My little brother never eats eggs. He has milk, bread and butter. For lunch we often have salad. We sometimes have pizza. On Sundays we sometimes go to a restaurant. Then I have beef, potatoes and carrots. My brother hates potatoes. He always has rice.

MORE fun with **Fido**

OK, let's have a barbecue.

Good idea!

Nice steaks!

????

Food from around the world

The food people eat in different countries depends on many different factors.

1 a **Look at the list below. What do you think are important factors?**

climate	money	national flag	culture
sport	religion	holidays	

Key words

export
produce
population
shrimp
olive oil
wheat
import
necessity
climate
commodity

b **Now read the text and check your answers.**

People eat different food in different countries. Why? There are many reasons. The climate can play a role. Hot, sunny places often grow more fruit and vegetables. People's religions and cultures are also important. Some religions do not eat certain foods. People also travel more these days so they try food from different countries. Of course, how much money you have also counts. If you haven't got much money, you can't always buy the best food.

2 a **What food can you see in the photos?**

b **What country do you think this food comes from? Compare your ideas with a partner.**

50 **3** **Look at the map. Write the numbers of the countries next to the names. Listen and check.**

☐ Brazil	☐ Egypt	☐ The USA
☐ China	☐ Ecuador	☐ Italy

4 **Listen to the dialogue and draw the symbols on the map.**

 chicken   rice   pasta   oranges   bananas   potatoes

International trade

Food is a necessity. We all need to eat. But food is also an important commodity for many countries. Countries can sell (export) their food to other countries or buy (import) food from other countries.

5 **Read the sentences. Which of the countries in Exercise 3 are they about?**

1 The capital city is Quito. People speak Spanish here. This country exports a lot of bananas and shrimps.

....

2 The capital city is Brasilia. People speak Portuguese here. This country produces and exports a lot of coffee, sugar and soya.

....

3 The capital city is Rome. This country produces a lot of olive oil and pasta.

....

4 The capital city is Cairo. People speak Arabic here. This country produces fresh fruit and vegetables.

....

5 The capital city is Washington DC. People speak English here. This country produces a lot of wheat and rice. It is famous for fast food.

....

6 The capital city is Beijing. This country has the biggest population in the world. People eat a lot of fish and rice.

....

Mini-project

6 **Tomorrow make a list of the food you eat. Find out where it came from. Write short texts like those in Exercise 5 about some of the countries. Then test your friends.**

e 100g

FREEZE-DRIED SOLUBLE COFFEE

Ingredients: 100% Coffee
Produce of more than one country
© 2008 Café Society Ltd. Cambridge
Best before end 06 2009

000521 675643

Geography

In this unit

You learn
- present simple (negatives and questions)
- object pronouns
- words for daily activities

and then you can
- ask and tell the time
- talk about routines

52 **1** **Listen and read.**

Nadia Hi, Kate. Would you like a crisp?

Kate No, thanks. I don't like them.

Nadia Oh dear! What's the matter with you today?

Kate I'm bored. My life's the same every day. I get up at seven o'clock, I have breakfast, I go to school, I have a boring lunch, I go home, I do my homework, then I have dinner, I listen to music and I go to bed at half past ten. The next day, I get up and do it again!

Nadia So what? What's the problem? It's the same for me.

Kate It's boring, boring, boring! I never go to interesting places. My parents don't understand me. And that good-looking boy Alain doesn't like me!

Nadia Hold on, Kate! Think about the *good* things in your life, like the French test tomorrow.

Kate Ha, ha! Do you know any *good* jokes? Oh, what's the time?

Nadia It's ten to six. Why?

Kate There's a great programme on TV at six o'clock. Do you want to watch it with me?

Nadia OK. But I hope it isn't boring!

2 **Circle the correct answer.**

1 Kate is *bored* / *happy* .
2 Kate gets up at *6.00* / *7.00* .
3 She goes to bed at *10.15* / *10.30* .
4 Kate's parents *understand* / *don't understand* her.
5 There's a French *lesson* / *test* at school tomorrow.

Get talking Asking and telling the time

 3 **Listen and read.**

It's three o'clock.

It's five past three.

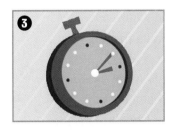

It's ten past three.

It's a quarter past three.

It's twenty past three.

It's twenty-five past three.

It's half past three.

It's twenty-five to four.

It's twenty to four.

It's a quarter to four.

It's ten to four.

It's five to four.

4 **Work with a partner. Cover a clock from Exercise 3 and ask and answer about the time.**

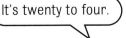

What's the time?   It's twenty to four.

Language Focus

Vocabulary Daily activities

54 **1** **Listen and write the phrases under the correct pictures.**

watch TV
play football
~~go shopping~~
do homework
listen to music
take the dog for
  a walk
go roller skating
hang out with
  friends
play computer
  games
read a book
play the piano
surf the Net

❶ ....*go shopping*....... **❷** .... **❸** .... **❹** ....

❺ .... **❻** .... **❼** .... **❽** ....

❾ .... **❿** .... **⓫** .... **⓬** ....

Get talking Talking about routines

55 **2** **Listen and tick the activities Ben and Lisa do.**

LISA
☐ take the dog for a walk
☐ do homework
☐ play football
☐ surf the Net
☐ go roller skating
☐ listen to music
☐ watch TV

BEN
☐ hang out with friends
☐ play computer games
☐ do homework
☐ read a book
☐ go roller skating
☐ go shopping
☐ listen to music

3 **Work in pairs. Talk about your day.**

A Saturday afternoons.

B Well, first I listen to music.

Grammar

Present simple Negative

 1 **Look at the dialogue on page 70 and complete the table.**

Present simple	Negative
I/you/we/they	[1]................. like them.
He/she/it	[2]................. like me.

2 **Rewrite the sentences using the negative form.**

1 I like tomatoes.
   I don't like tomatoes.........................

2 He hates football.
   ....

3 We know the answer.
   ....

4 You tell good jokes.
   ....

5 They live here.
   ....

6 My brother watches TV every day.
   ....

7 Nadia goes shopping on Fridays.
   ....

8 Our teacher does homework.
   ....

3 **Write the negative form of the verb to complete the sentences.**

1 I .....*don't speak*..... Spanish. (speak)
2 We .... meat on Fridays. (eat)
3 My father .... ice cream. (like)
4 They .... TV at the weekend. (watch)
5 I'm sorry – I .... (understand)
6 Steve .... the Net. (surf)
7 She .... the answer. (know)
8 Adrian and Mary .... in a big house. (live)

Present simple Questions and short answers

 4 **Look at the dialogue on page 70 and complete the table.**

Questions		
[1]...........	I/you/we/they	get up at 6?
Does	he/she/it	go to bed at 9 o'clock?

Short answers	
Positive	Yes, I/you/we/they **do**.
	Yes, he/she/it **does**.
Negative	No, I/you/we/they **don't**.
	No, he/she/it **doesn't**.

5 **Write questions and short answers.**

1 he / play football? (✓)
   Does he play football........................?
   Yes, he does.........................

2 they / watch TV on Fridays? (✗)
   ....?
   ....

3 you / eat fruit? (✓)
   ....?
   ....

4 she / go shopping at the weekend? (✓)
   ....?
   ....

5 Steve and Nadia / speak Italian? (✗)
   ....?
   ....

6 you / like romantic films? (✗)
   ....?
   ....

Get talking Talking about daily routines

6
56
Listen to the interview with Nick and Melanie. Draw the times they do each activity on the clocks below.

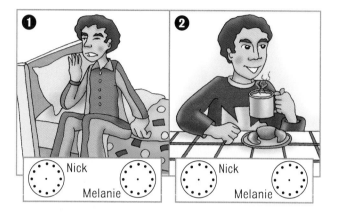

Object pronouns

7 Use the words below to complete the table.

> him   them   us   me
> her   you   it

Object pronouns		
Subject pronoun		Object pronoun
I	→	1 ....
you	→	2 ....
he	→	3 ....
she	→	4 ....
it	→	5 ....
we	→	6 ....
they	→	7 ....

8 Circle the correct object pronoun to complete the sentences.

1 This is Mark. Do you know *him* / *her* ?
2 They are Chinese. I speak to *them* / *it* every day.
3 That's my house. Do you like *it* / *her* ?
4 I'm Maria. Talk to *me* / *him* .
5 We are Spanish but my English friend lives with *us* / *them* .

9 Complete with the correct object pronoun.

1 This is my new computer. Do you like ...*it*..?
2 There's Steve. Let's talk to ....
3 We play football every Sunday. Come and play with ....!
4 Jennifer Aniston's on TV. Do you like ....?
5 I go to bed at 10 – please phone .... before then.

Reading

1 **Read the text.**

A Day in the Life of **Christina** *and* **Suresh**

Hi, I'm Christina. I live on a farm in Texas. I get up at half past seven. At a quarter to eight, I go and feed my horse. At a quarter past eight, I have breakfast with my family. At twenty to nine, my mother takes me to school by car. School starts at nine o'clock. School ends at four o'clock. My mother picks me up and then we often go shopping. When I come home, I ride my horse for an hour. Then I do my homework or watch TV. Our family has dinner at half past seven. Then I phone my friends or work on my computer. Before I go to sleep, I read for half an hour. I go to bed at ten o'clock or half past ten.

I'm Suresh. I live with my mother in a village in India. The big city is six hours away by bus. My mother and I get up at five o'clock in the morning. My mother goes out to cut grass for our water buffalos. I go and get water from the river. At six o'clock, I cook breakfast for my baby brother and for my mother. At half past six, I leave for school. I walk to school from half past six to eight o'clock. School begins at eight o'clock and ends at half past two. I walk home and then I go out to cut grass for the buffalos. Then I clean the buffalo shed. We go to bed early, very often at half past eight or nine o'clock.

2 **Tick the correct times for the activities.**

1 Christina gets up at ....

2 Suresh gets up at ....

3 At .... Christina has breakfast.

4 At .... Suresh cooks breakfast.

5 At .... Christina goes to school.

6 Suresh leaves for school at ....

7 Christina's family has dinner at ....

8 Suresh's school ends at ....

A song 4 U The master of time

o'clock
quarter
half past (x 3)
twelve
clock (x 2)

The master of time!

*I'm the master, the
master of time. (x 2)*

*Chorus (x 2)
Listen, I'm
the master of time, (x 2)
and here's my rhyme.*

*Six ¹................,
let's play some rock.
Ten past eight – oh, dear,
I'm late
²................ three,
slap your knee.
From ³................ to one,
let's have some fun.*

*I'm the master,
the master of time (x 2)*

*One to three, rock with me
a ⁴................ past,
this is too fast.
⁵................ ten,
and this is when
I hear a knock my good old ⁶................ .*

Chorus

*⁷................ ten, and this is when
I hear a knock my good old
⁸................ . (x 2)
One last hop, we have to stop.*

Chorus (x 1)

*Listen, I'm the master of time,
the master of time and here, my friend,
is the end, of my rhyme, my rhyme.
Oh, yeah, baby!*

Writing for your Portfolio

4 | **Read the text and describe your day.**

A day in the life of Sarah Brown

I get up at seven. I have breakfast at a quarter past seven.
I go to school at a quarter to eight. Our school starts at eight
o'clock and it ends at half past twelve. In the afternoon, I play
with my friends, I read or I listen to music. Then I do my homework.
I often watch TV from six to eight. At nine o'clock I go to bed.

MORE fun with **Fido**

Time for work.

Time for school.

Time for lunch!

Check your progress Units 5 and 6

1 **Write two words for each category.**

1 vegetables ....
2 drinks ....
3 fruit ....
4 meat ....

☐ 8

2 **Put the sentences in order to form a dialogue.**

.... I'd like a steak, please.
.... What would you like to eat?
.... No, thanks. I don't like them.
.... Can I have potatoes?
.... Of course. Would you like carrots, too?
.... What vegetables would you like?

☐ 6

3 **Tick the correct sentences and correct the wrong ones.**

1 I eat fruit never. ☐

....

2 They always go to bed at 10 o'clock. ☐

....

3 My teacher often is late for class. ☐

....

4 We sometimes go to the cinema with Jack. ☐

....

5 He watches usually TV after dinner. ☐

☐ 5

4 **Rewrite the sentences using the negative form.**

1 I go to the gym every day.

....

2 Sue and Belinda like ice cream.

....

3 Nadia wants chicken and chips.

....

4 My mother drinks a lot of tea.

....

5 School finishes at 4 o'clock.

....

☐ 10

5 **Match the words.**

1 play   a shopping
2 listen   b for a walk
3 hang out   c a book
4 go   d to music
5 read   e TV
6 watch   f the piano
7 take the dog g with friends

☐ 7

6 **Complete the dialogues with object pronouns.**

1 **A** Do you want to watch Big Brother tonight?
  B No, thanks. I don't like ....
2 **A** Would you like to talk to Charles?
  B Yes, I would. Let's phone ....
3 **A** Are you at home tonight?
  B Yes. Phone .... at 9 o'clock.
4 **A** Why haven't you got dogs at your house?
  B Because we don't like ....

☐ 4

7 **Answer the questions.**

1 What time do you get up?

....

2 When does your school begin?

....

3 Do you go to school by bus?

....

4 Do you have homework every day?

....

5 Do you play football after school?

....

☐ 10

TOTAL ☐ 50

My progress so far is ...

☺ **brilliant!** ☐

😐 **quite good.** ☐

☹ **not great.** ☐

Multicultural Britain

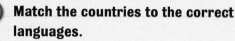

DISTRICTS OF LONDON

1 Match the countries to the correct languages.

1	France	a	Spanish
2	Iran	b	Vietnamese
3	Turkey	c	Greek
4	Brazil & Portugal	d	Albanian
5	India	e	French
6	Vietnam	f	Turkish
7	Spain & Mexico	g	Farsi
8	Egypt	h	Arabic
9	Albania	i	Portuguese
10	Greece	j	Hindi & English

FACT FILE

FOCUS ON LONDON

Haringey is a district in London. It has got 67 primary schools and 22 secondary schools. Pupils in Haringey are from countries all over the world. They speak 190 different languages.

Languages

English Turkish Bengali French Albanian Arabic Portuguese Farsi Urdu Greek Spanish Vietnamese

2 Read the texts and answer the questions.

TALKING ABOUT MUSIC

NAME Gursharan Singh
NATIONALITY Indian
HOME London

In London today, Bhangra is very popular. Bhangra is a new trend in dance music but it is originally a folk dance from Punjab in India. Modern Bhangra is a mixture of hip-hop, reggae, house, and drum-and-bass. My favourite artists are Missy Elliot, Jay Sean and Panjabi MC.

NAME Zeynep Aksu
NATIONALITY Turkish
HOME London

Turkish pop music is big in the Turkish community here. It has got a different sound from other European pop music. It's a mixture of Eastern and Western music. My favourite pop singer is Tarkan. He's very good-looking! Rafet el Roman, Sertab Erener and Aşkın Nur Yengi are good singers too.

1 What sort of music is Bhangra?
2 What is Turkish pop music like?
3 Where is Bhangra from originally?
4 Who is Tarkan?

3 Listen to the interview and complete the text.

Name *Manuel Bautista*   **Nationality** *Mexican*   **Home** *London*

Manuel is from [1]........................ but his family is from [2]........................ . His favourite [3]........................ is salsa. Salsa [4]........................ popular in London. It is [5]........................ and it has got a strong dance beat. His [6]........................ musician is his dad. He is a [7]........................ in a salsa band. There are a lot of salsa [8]........................ in London. Salsa music and dance are very popular.

4 **Over 2 U!** Interview a partner and write a paragraph about their favourite music.

MORE! And now you can watch *Kids in the UK!*

The world's best detective

Detective Case is at home. The telephone rings.

> Hello, Detective Case — the world's best detective.

> This is Lady Grey. Please help me find my cat, Pepper. I don't know where he is.

> Don't worry, Lady Grey.

Detective Case leaves his house. He looks for Pepper. He comes to a bridge.

> Perhaps Pepper is under the bridge.

He looks under the bridge. Pepper isn't there. Case falls into the river.

Detective Case goes to the park. He looks for Pepper — but he bumps into a tree.

> Perhaps Pepper is in the park.

> OK. Perhaps Pepper is in the woods.

Detective Case goes to the woods. He looks for Pepper, but he sees — a wolf!

Detective Case climbs a tree and sits in it. He watches the wolf. He's very scared. He hears a noise. He looks around, and he sees — Pepper!

Detective Case is very happy. He picks Pepper up and phones Lady Grey.

> Hello? Lady Grey? I'm in the woods. I've got Pepper.

> Wonderful!

> But I've got a problem. There's a wolf here. Please help me!

> Give me twenty minutes!

For **MORE!** Go to www.cambridge.org/elt/more to check the ending of the story. Do a quiz on this text.

UNIT 6   79

In this unit

You learn
- demonstrative adjectives and pronouns
- countable and uncountable nouns
- *How much?/How many?*
- *some/any*
- words for clothes

and then you can
- talk about prices
- talk about clothes

59

1 Listen and read.

Jack	This is boring!
Nadia	Jack, there's a party tonight and I want some new clothes.
Kate	Do you like this top?
Nadia	No, not really. But that top's nice. How much is it?
Kate	Let's see. It's ... £12.99.
Steve	That's expensive. How much money have you got, Nadia?
Nadia	£25. My granny always gives me some money for my birthday.
Jack	Lucky you! I haven't got a rich granny!

Kate	Look Nadia – these trousers are nice. Oh, there's no price on them.
Nadia	Excuse me – how much are those trousers?
Assistant	They're £29.99.
Nadia	Thanks. Oh dear, I've only got £25!
Steve	Don't worry, I can lend you £5.
Nadia	Thanks, Steve! Excuse me – can I try these trousers on, please?
Assistant	Sure. The changing rooms are over there.
Steve	Come on, Jack. I'm hungry. Let's go and buy some food. Oh no! Now I haven't got any money!

2 **Correct the wrong information in each sentence.**

1 There's a ~~football match~~ tonight.   ...*party*....
2 Kate wants some new clothes.   ....
3 The top is £12.50.   ....
4 Nadia's got £50.   ....
5 Nadia's mother gives her money on her birthday.   ....
6 The trousers are £19.99.   ....

Get talking Talking about prices

60 **3** **Listen and repeat.**

£28 $39   €47   £52   £65 $73   £81   €99   €100

61 **4** **Guess the prices of the objects then listen and read.**

£8.99   £179.00   £34.99   £16.99   £3.50   £5.00
99p   £9.99   £2.50   £1.99   £69.99   £34.99

I think the key-ring is…

I think the mobile phone is…

I think the sweets are…

1 T-shirt
2 magazine
3 dog food
5 sweets
4 mobile phone
6 MP3 player
7 computer game
8 key-ring
10 book
9 DVD and CD
11 jeans

62 **5** **Listen to the dialogues in the shop and practise them in pairs.**

Dialogue 1

Boy   How much are the trainers?
Shop assistant They're £29.99.
Boy   And the T-shirt?
Shop assistant It's £6.99. Or two for £9.99.
Boy   Thank you.

Dialogue 2

Shop assistant Yes, please?
Girl   How much is the DVD? There's no price on it.
Shop assistant They're all £12.99.
Girl   Thank you.

Language Focus

Vocabulary Clothes

63 **1** **Look, listen and repeat.**

(a pair of) socks
cap
skirt
(a pair of) shoes
T-shirt
(a pair of) trousers
(a pair of) trainers
dress
shirt
jacket
(a pair of) jeans
sweater

2 **Work with a partner. Close your books and ask and answer questions about the colour of the clothes in the picture.**

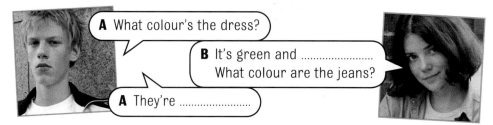

A What colour's the dress?

B It's green and ....
What colour are the jeans?

A They're ....

Get talking Talking about clothes

3 **Interview a partner.**

Do you buy your own clothes?
Do you wear T-shirts with pictures on?
Do you wear jeans with holes?
How many pairs of shoes have you got?

No, I don't.

Yes, I do.

About six, I think.

Grammar

Demonstrative adjectives and pronouns

1 **Read the dialogue on page 80 and complete the sentences.**

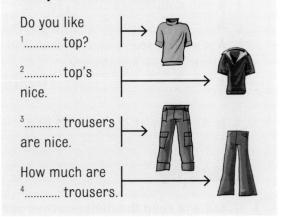

Do you like
¹............ top?

²............ top's nice.

³............ trousers are nice.

How much are
⁴............ trousers.

2 **Complete with _this_, _that_, _these_, or _those_.**

1 I like .... cheese.

2 Look at .... dog. It's going into the shop.

3 Who are .... boys?

4 How much are .... cherries?

Countable and uncountable nouns

3 **Look at the examples and choose the correct option to complete the rule.**

Countable: boy**s**, hous**es**, trouser**s**, top**s**.
Uncountable: money, food, ham. (NOT: ~~moneys, foods, hams~~)

✳ We _do_ / _do not_ add an –s to uncountable nouns to make them plural.

4 **Write U next to the uncountable nouns and C next to the countable ones.**

1 money _U_
2 book _C_
3 cheese ......
4 sandwich ......
5 man ......
6 bread ......
7 water ......
8 homework ......

How much?/How many?

5 **Read the examples and complete the rule with _How much_ and _How many_.**

How much money have you got?
How many T-shirts have you got?

✳ We use ¹.............. with countable nouns.
✳ We use ².............. with uncountable nouns.

6 **Circle the correct word.**

1 How _much_ / _many_ books have you got?
2 How _much_ / _many_ food is there in the fridge?
3 How _much_ / _many_ children are in your class?
4 How _much_ / _many_ water do you drink every day?
5 How _much_ / _many_ sandwiches do you want?
6 How _much_ / _many_ apple juice would you like?
7 How _much_ / _many_ money have you got?
8 How _much_ / _many_ pairs of shoes has she got?

some/any

7 **Look at the examples and complete the rules with _some_ or _any_.**

I haven't got **any** nice clothes.
Have you got **any** money?
She always gives me **some** money.
I want **some** new trousers.

＊ With uncountable and countable plural nouns:
use [1]........................ in positive sentences.
use [2]........................ in negative sentences.
use [3]........................ in questions.

8 **Complete the sentences with _some_ or _any_.**

1 I'd like ....*some*...... water, please.
2 Are there .... bananas in the kitchen?
3 We haven't got .... food in the house!
4 Our mother often gives us .... money at the weekend.
5 There are .... great DVDs in that shop.
6 Have you got .... good games on your computer?
7 There's .... apple juice on the table.
8 I've got .... homework to do tonight.

9 **Write _some, any, much_ or _many_. Then listen and check.**

1 **A** Have you got .... brothers or sisters?
  B No, I haven't.
2 **A** How .... money is there?
  B £22.
3 **A** How .... CDs have you got?
  B 60, I think.
4 **A** What would you like in your tea?
  B .... sugar please, but no milk.
5 **A** I would like .... chicken. And you?
  B No, thanks. I don't want .... chicken.
6 **A** How .... children are there in your class?
  B There are 16 girls, and 12 boys.

Listening

10 **Listen and read the dialogue then act it out in pairs.**

65

Assistant Can I help you?
Boy Yes, please. I'd like some running shoes. How much are these shoes here?
Assistant They aren't for running. They're for basketball.
Boy Alright. What about those green shoes over there?
Assistant I'm sorry. They're for volleyball.
Boy And those blue shoes in the box over there?
Assistant They're for cycling.
Boy Right. Where are the shoes for running?
Assistant Well, these shoes are for running in the woods, and those shoes there are ...
Boy Alright. Stop it, please! I'd like a T-shirt.
Assistant For basketball? For volleyball? For football? This T-shirt is for basketball. And that T-shirt over there is for beach volleyball. And that blue T-shirt is for running. What would you like?
Boy I'd like to go home now. And watch the sport on TV! Goodbye.

Skills

Listening

66 **1** **Listen and circle T (True) or F (False).**

1 The man and the woman buy some cheese. T / F
2 They buy two hundred grammes. T / F
3 They buy four slices of meat. T / F
4 They also buy some bottles of carrot juice. T / F
5 They don't buy any bottles of apple juice. T / F
6 The man and the woman haven't got a fridge. T / F

2 **Complete the dialogue with the expressions on the left.**

That's all.
How many
    bottles?
Anything else?
I'd like some
How many?
How much?

Man	Good morning.
Shopkeeper	Good morning.
Man	¹..
	cheddar cheese, please.
Shopkeeper	²..
Man	A hundred grammes.
Shopkeeper	OK, a hundred grammes of cheese. ³...........................
	....
Man	I'd also like some eggs.

Shopkeeper	⁴..
Man	Four.
Shopkeeper	Anything else?
Man	Some orange juice, please.
Shopkeeper	⁵..
Man	Six.
Shopkeeper	Anything else?
Man	No, thank you. ⁶.................... ....

Speaking

3 **Work in groups of three. You are at the market and want to buy some of these products: sausages, oranges, apples, strawberries, grapes, onions, tomatoes, bread and cheese.**

We'd like some lemons, please.

How many?

Reading

 Read the story.

THE HORSE CAN COUNT

1 Joe rides into town on his horse Jolly. Today he wants to buy a lot of things for the winter. There's only one shop in town. It's Old Fred's shop. Joe goes into the shop.

Fred says, 'Hi, Joe! Good to see you. What can I do for you today?'

'Hi, Fred,' says Joe, 'Well, first, I'd like some beans.'

'Right. Beans. How many?'

'40 kilos, and some rice.'

'How much rice?'

'30 kilos.'

40+30+80 =150...

2 'Next, I'd like some potatoes.'

'How many bags?'

'Eight,' Joe says.

'No problem. Anything else?' asks Fred.

'No, thanks,' says Joe.

Jolly hears Joe and Fred. He thinks: '40 kilos of beans and 30 kilos of rice. *And* eight bags of potatoes. That's 80 kilos! 40 kilos and 30 kilos and 80 kilos are *150 kilos!* No way! Joe can carry them – not me!' And Jolly gallops back home.

3 Ten minutes later, Joe comes out of the shop. Jolly isn't there. When Joe arrives back at the farm, Jolly is under the big apple tree.

5 ÷ 5 = 1
'Five kilometres in five hours. Man, that's slow!'

---

5 **Number the sentences in the order of the story.**

- [ ] Jolly listens to Joe and Fred.
- [ ] Jolly gallops home to the farm.
- [ ] Jolly doesn't want to carry 150 kilos.
- [ ] Joe rides into town.
- [ ] Joe buys beans, rice and potatoes.
- [ ] Joe wants to buy things in Fred's shop.
- [ ] Five hours and ten minutes later Joe gets back to the farm.

6 **Read the text and try and solve the problem.**

A man rides into town on Friday. He stays two nights and leaves on Saturday. How is this possible?

Sounds right /ð/

 7 **Listen and repeat.**

This blue shirt and these green socks —
I can put them in this box!
Those black trousers, that red sweater —
In the drawer? Yes, that's better!

Speaking

8 **Think of someone in the class. Work with a partner. Ask and answer questions about them.**

Does he sometimes wear jeans?

Yes, he does.

Does he often wear brown shoes?

No, he doesn't.

Does he always wear T-shirts?

Yes, he does.

Is it John?

Yes, it is.

Writing for your Portfolio

9 **Read the text and describe the clothes you like to wear.**

Hi, I'm Susan. I often wear blue jeans, blue socks and blue and white trainers. My favourite sweater is pink. There is a picture of a horse on it. I like jeans, but I don't like skirts or trousers.

Hi, I'm...
I often / sometimes / never wear...
My favourite ... is ...
I like...., but I don't like...

MORE fun with Fido

Maths made easy

Key words

key in	subtract	divide (by)
add	multiply (by)	divisible (by)

1 Work with a partner. Find the answer to the puzzle.

> **A girl asks a zookeeper,**
>
> 'How many camels and parrots are there in your zoo?'
> The man says, 'Good question.
> Together they've got 60 eyes and 86 feet!'
> The girl is very clever.
> She finds the answer in 10 minutes!
>
> **Can you find the answer?**

Tip: think about the eyes first!

2 Try this calculator trick. Work in pairs. Give your partner a calculator and tell him/her to do these things:

- Key in the number of the month of your birthday
- Multiply by 4
- Add 13
- Multiply by 25
- Subtract 200
- Add the number of the day of your birthday
- Multiply by 2
- Subtract 40
- Multiply by 50
- Add the last two digits of the year of your birthday
- Subtract 10500
- Show me the calculator. Your date of birth is …

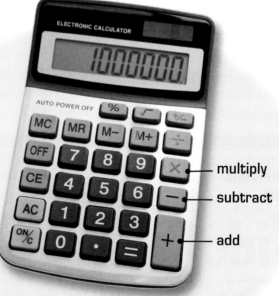

multiply
subtract
add

Tip: The first one or two digits give the month, the next two give the day, the last two the year!

Answer to number 1: There are 17 parrots and 13 camels

3 **a** **Read the texts about shortcuts.**

Maths shortcuts

Look: 9 ÷ 3 = 3 (9 is divisible by 3)

Is a number divisible by 3? It's easy to find out.
Add up the digits. Divide the sum by 3.
Is it possible? → The number is divisible by 3.
Is it not possible? → The number is not divisible by 3.

Examples:
379428   3 + 7 + 9 + 4 + 2 + 8 = 33 (divisible by 3!)
610894   6 + 1 + 0 + 8 + 9 + 4 = 28 (not divisible!)

Is a number divisible by 9?

Add up the digits. Divide the sum by 9. Is it possible?
Yes? → The number is divisible by 9.
No? → The number is not divisible by 9.

Dividing or multiplying by 5 is easy!

Remember that 5 is half of ten.
To multiply 5 x 86, work out 10 x 86 first: 860.
Then divide in half: 430
To divide 98 by 5, divide by ten first: 9.8
Then double the answer: 19.6

Is a number divisible by 5?

Look at the last digit.
Is it 5 or 0? → The number is divisible by 5.

Is a number divisible by 4?

Look at the last 2 digits.

- Are they 00? → The number is divisible by 4.
  4598376589997800 Yes!

- Is the last two-digit number divisible by 4?
  3564785476899936 Yes!
  36 ÷ 4 = 9
  Yes → The whole number is divisible by 4.

Multiplying by 11 is easy!

Remember that 11 = 10 + 1.
To multiply 49 x 11,
multiply 49 x 10 first: 490.
Then add 49: 490 + 49 = 539

b **Can you think of more shortcuts? Tell your class.**

Mini-project

4 **Work with a partner.**

a **Tick the answers to these questions. Do not use a calculator.**

1 Is 23 divisible by 3? ☐ Yes ☐ No
2 Is 2905 divisible by 5? ☐ Yes ☐ No
3 Is 34987465 divisible by 9? ☐ Yes ☐ No
4 Is 75938627824 divisible by 4? ☐ Yes ☐ No
5 Is 9427211163291 divisible by 3? ☐ Yes ☐ No
6 Is 45879435768903212873 divisible by 9? ☐ Yes ☐ No

b **Find the answers to these questions quickly.**

1 How much is 73 x 11?
2 How much is 5 x 99?
3 How much is 128 divided by 5?

5 **With your partner, write a quiz for another pair of students.**

UNIT (8) My family

In this unit

You learn
- *can* for ability
- *can* questions and short answers
- *like/love/hate doing*
- words for family members

and then you can
- talk about abilities
- talk about things you like doing
- ask for permission
- talk about family

68

1 **Listen and read.**

Nadia Is this your photo album, Kate?

Kate Yes, it is.

Nadia Can I have a look? I love looking at photos.

Kate Sure. Here you are. They're from my granny's birthday party. She's 80.

Nadia She looks great for 80.

Kate Yes. She's fine, but she can't walk without a stick.

Nadia And who's that next to your granny?

Kate That's my uncle Jeremy. He likes telling jokes. Look at the big smile on Granny's face.

Nadia Oh yes. And who's that?

Kate That's my cousin Ellen. I don't really like her.

Nadia Why not?

Kate I can't really say. She's so perfect, you know. She can speak three languages and play two instruments, and she's everybody's darling.

Nadia I see. Do you like meeting up with all your family? All your uncles and aunts and cousins and your grandparents?

Kate Yes, I do.

Nadia And your parents?

Kate They like it, too. As long as it isn't at our house!

2 Circle T (True) or F (False) for the sentences below.

1 Nadia loves looking at photos. T / F
2 Kate's grandmother is 80. T / F
3 Kate's grandmother can't walk without a stick. T / F
4 Kate's uncle Jeremy doesn't like jokes. T / F
5 Ellen can speak two languages. T / F
6 Ellen's everybody's darling. T / F
7 Kate likes Ellen. T / F
8 Kate doesn't like family meetings. T / F

Get talking Asking for permission

3 Listen and repeat.

A Can I go to the toilet, please?
B Yes, of course.

A Can I open the window?
B No, please don't.

A Can I borrow your pen?
B Sure, here you are.

A Can I borrow your computer?
B Sorry, it doesn't work.

4 Work with a partner. Invent dialogues using the pictures.

Language Focus

Vocabulary Family members

70 **1** **Listen and write the names in the correct box.**

William
Natasha
Anthony
Susan
Fred
Juliette
Lisa

grandmother

grandfather

aunt

uncle

mother

father

cousin

Ben

Get talking Talking about family

2 **Ask and answer.**

A Who's Ben's father?

B William is Ben's father.

3 **Work with a partner. Write the names of some of your relatives (mother, father, uncle etc). Give the list to your partner. Your partner asks you who they are.**

A Who's Susanne?

B She's my aunt.

A Who are Cindy and Jane?

B They're my cousins.

Grammar

Can for ability

	+/−	
I/you/we/they/ he/she/it	**can/can't**	speak French.

Can is the same for all subjects/people.

1 **Complete the sentences with *can* and one of the forms of the verb.**

1 He ...*can play*... the piano. (play / playing)
2 I .... on my head. (stand / standing)
3 John .... four languages. (speaks / speak)
4 My brothers .... horses. (riding / ride)

2 **Complete the sentences with *can* or *can't*.**

1 She ...*can*... speak French, but she can't speak Spanish.
2 He is very tired. He .... play football now.
3 My little sister is very musical. She .... sing and play the piano.
4 My grandpa is 85. He is very fit, but he .... ride a bike.
5 I .... stand on my head! Isn't this great?
6 Please help me look for my pen. I .... find it!

Can Questions and short answers

Questions		
Can	I/you/we/they/he/she/it	speak French?
✓	Yes, I/you/we/they/he/she/it	**can**.
✗	No, I/you/we/they/he/she/it	**can't**.

3 **Answer the questions about you.**

1 Can you play the piano?
....
2 Can you speak Spanish?
....

3 Can you ride a horse?
....
4 Can you stand on your head?
....
5 Can you make a cake?
....
6 Can you run for two hours?
....

4 **Listen and complete.**

 juggle   nose   ears   head   climb   hands

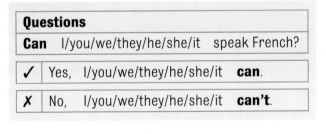

1 wiggle your
....

2 stand on your
....

3 walk on your
....

4 touch your
.... with your tongue

5 ....

6 ....
a tree

Get talking Talking about abilities

5 **Say what you *can* and *can't* do.**

I can ...., but I can't ....

6 **Interview your partner about what they *can* and *can't* do.**

A Can you ....?

B Yes, I can.

C No, I can't.

Like/love/hate doing

7 **Look at the dialogue on page 90 and complete the sentences.**

I love ¹.................... at photos.
He likes ².................... jokes.
Do you like ³.................... up with all your family?

✳ After the verbs *like/love/hate* we often use verb + *ing*

8 **Reorder the words and make sentences.**

1 doesn't / going / like / she / cinema / to the
   She doesn't like going to the cinema. ....

2 playing / computer games / hates / Gerry
   ....

3 my / likes / watching / sister / westerns
   ....

4 friends / to music / love / my / listening
   ....

9 **Complete the sentences with one of the verbs on the left.**

speak
watch
meet up
~~listen to~~
tell
do

1 I love ....*listening to*.... hip-hop music. It's fantastic!
2 We hate .... homework. It's difficult and boring.
3 My dad likes .... old films on TV.
4 Giula loves .... jokes. She's very funny!
5 Do you like .... English?
6 They love .... with their friends in town on Saturdays.

Reading

1 Read the text. Write the name of the person who does each activity below the correct picture.

The Boehmer Family

The Boehmer family are a large family. There are the parents, Larry and Judy, and there are eleven children – seven girls and four boys. All of the Boehmer family are jugglers and they do shows all over the USA, even the dog, Bosco, is part of the show.

Every week they practise for 8 to10 hours for their shows. Of, course they are also interested in other things. Adam, the eldest son,

likes working out, and Casey, the eldest daughter, likes water-skiing and running. Sarah and Melissa like rollerblading, Margaret the youngest, likes riding her horses, and Rebecca likes learning new juggling tricks.

They all love doing the shows. 'It's not very difficult', Larry says. 'Anybody can do it. Practice and more practice – that's the secret. And don't get lazy.'

....

2 Reread the text and say if the sentences are **T (True)** or **F (False)**.

1 There are eleven people in the Boehmer family. T / F
2 The family have a pet. T / F
3 They practise 8 to 10 hours every day. T / F
4 Larry thinks juggling is difficult. T / F

Listening

3 Listen and tick the activities you hear.

playing basketball   swimming   dancing   going shopping

climbing a tree   reading   playing tennis   talking to my friends on the phone

A Song 4 U Heaven

 4 Complete the song with the words. Then listen, check and sing.

listen
hear
sing
take
play

¹.......... me by the hand.
².......... to our band.
Let the music rock.
Sing around the clock.

Chorus (x 2)
With Project Eleven,
you are in heaven.
Yes, you are in heaven,
with Project Eleven.

Let's ³.......... the guitar.
⁴.......... the drums from far.
Let the keyboards rock.
⁵.......... around the clock.

Writing for your Portfolio

5 Read the poem and write one for yourself. Draw a picture.

This is me.
I can speak French, German, English and Italian.
I love singing.
I can play the piano, the guitar and the drums.
I love playing music.
I can write with my left and my right hand.
But I don't like writing!

 **MORE fun with Fido**

'Take me by the hand.'

Check your progress Units 7 and 8

1 Write the name of the clothes.

1 redss .... 4 kacjte ....
2 krits .... 5 ksocs ....
3 osrretus .... 6 rtnieasr ....

☐ 6

2 Complete the table.

father	
	grandmother
uncle	
	cousin

☐ 4

3 Complete the sentences with the correct form of the verb.

1 I like .... (wear) jeans.
2 Daisy can .... (speak) Russian.
3 Harry hates .... (go) to bed early.
4 We don't like .... (listen) to classical music.
5 Mary can't .... (come) to school today.
6 My parents love .... (play) golf.

☐ 6

4 Circle the correct word.

1 I love *this / those* new trousers.
2 How *much / many* homework have you got?
3 Are there *some / any* English people in your town?
4 We don't like *this / these* new CD.
5 I haven't got *some / any* money at the moment.
6 How *much / many* pairs of shoes has he got?

☐ 6

5 Put the sentences in order to make a dialogue.

...... Yes, please. How much are these jeans?
...... Thanks. Can I try them on, please?
.... Can I help you?
...... They're £60.
...... Of course. The changing rooms are over there.
...... Thank you.

☐ 6

6 Complete the dialogue.

How many	How much	some
any	those	I help you

SA   Hello! Can [1].......................... ?
Girl Yes, I'd like [2].......................... salami, please.
SA   [3].......................... would you like?
Girl Six slices, please. Have you got [4].......................... sausages?
SA   Yes, I've got [5].......................... nice ones over there. [6].......................... do you want?
Girl Six, please.

☐ 6

7 Write the answers to the questions.

1 Can you ride a horse? (✓) ....
2 Can I borrow a blue pen, please? (✓)
....
3 Can I open the window? (✗) ....
4 Can Thomas speak Japanese? (✗)
....
5 Can your friends come tomorrow? (✓)
....
6 Can your dad run fast? (✗) ....

☐ 6

8 Answer the questions.

1 Can you swim? ....
2 Do you like going to school?
....
3 Do you wear caps?
....
4 How many CDs have you got?
....
5 How much money have you got?
....

☐ 10

TOTAL ☐ 50

My progress so far is ...

☺ **brilliant!** ☐
😐 **quite good.** ☐
☹ **not great.** ☐

School breakfast clubs

1 **Read the text about Breakfast Clubs in schools.**

A healthy start to the day

Hi, I'm Ayshe and I'm eleven years old. I go to a school in Devon in the south-west of England. We've got a breakfast club at school. A lot of schools have got them now. Our breakfast club is very popular. The favourite breakfast is Coco Pops and toast. However, not everybody eats Coco Pops and toast. My friend Dipak's favourite breakfast is fried eggs, sausage and beans – not very healthy! Fried food is bad for you. My friend, Karen, likes fruit for breakfast. She's a healthy eater. Me … I like everything. Check out our menu below.

FACT FILE

Why do schools in England have breakfast clubs?

- some children don't have breakfast at home. Then they are hungry.
- children often arrive early at school because both their parents work.
- children eat unhealthy snacks like sweets, chocolate and fizzy drinks for breakfast.

2 **Circle T (True) or F (False) for the sentences below.**

1 Ayshe goes to school in the north-west of England. T / F
2 People like the breakfast club. T / F
3 Coco Pops and toast are popular. T / F
4 Dipak always eats a healthy breakfast. T / F
5 Karen doesn't like fruit. T / F

3 **Write the name of each food.**

The Breakfast Club Menu

fruit
milk
fruit juice
sausages
boiled egg
baked beans
cornflakes
fried egg
coco pops
toast
tea

4 **Listen and write what Nathan eats and drinks.**

Eats: .... Drinks: ....

5 **Over 2 U!** **Write a menu for a Breakfast Club at your school.**

MORE! And now you can watch *Kids in the UK!*

Learn **MORE** about culture

Teenage web designer

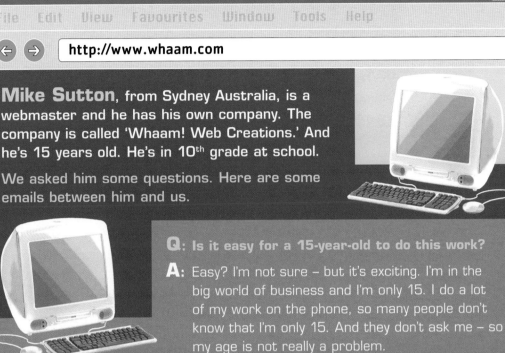

File   Edit   View   Favourites   Window   Tools   Help

http://www.whaam.com

Mike Sutton, from Sydney Australia, is a webmaster and he has his own company. The company is called 'Whaam! Web Creations.' And he's 15 years old. He's in 10th grade at school.

We asked him some questions. Here are some emails between him and us.

Q: Is it easy for a 15-year-old to do this work?

A: Easy? I'm not sure – but it's exciting. I'm in the big world of business and I'm only 15. I do a lot of my work on the phone, so many people don't know that I'm only 15. And they don't ask me – so my age is not really a problem.

Q: How do you learn the things you need to know?

A: Experience! It's the best way to learn things, I think. Sometimes I have a problem and I look at other pages on the Web to find answers. I've got friends, too, who can help me sometimes.

Q: What is the importance of the Internet for people?

A: I don't think it is very important, really. It's wonderful, of course – it's so easy to get information. But I don't think it's a very important thing in the world.

Q: Do you do your own programming and design?

A: Usually, yes. It's fun. But I also have some good people who do work for me. They're all very creative people.

Q: What does the Internet offer young people?

A: It's brilliant for young people. They can find friends and do interesting work. But it's slow sometimes, and that's a problem.

For **MORE!** Go to www.cambridge.org/elt/more and do a quiz on this text.

In this unit

You learn
- present continuous
- forming words with *-ing*
- telephone numbers
- ordinal numbers
- months of the year

and then you can
- talk on the phone
- talk about birthdays

4

1 Listen and read.

Kate Hello? Kate speaking.

Nadia Hi, Kate. It's Nadia here. How are things?

Kate OK. I'm doing some homework and I'm not enjoying it!

Nadia Oh sorry. Am I disturbing you?

Kate No, you aren't. It's OK.

Nadia Oh good. Listen – have you got Jack's phone number?

Kate Yeah, I have. Just a moment. Ready? It's 8693 2210.

Nadia 8693 2210. Thanks.

Kate Why do you want Jack's number?

Nadia It's Steve's birthday next weekend, on the 16th. I want to buy him something.

Kate Ah, clever you! You want to ask Jack what Steve likes.

Nadia That's right.

Kate OK. But you can't talk to him now. He's playing football. Phone him after lunch.

Nadia Oh dear. I really need to talk to him now!

Kate Why? Are you trying to find something now?

Nadia Yes, I am. I'm in a bookshop and … oh, oh! Kate, can I phone you back?

Kate Sure, why?

Nadia Steve's coming into the shop! Bye!

Kate Bye, Nadia!

2 Circle the correct words or expressions.

1 Kate is *writing letters* / *doing homework* .
2 Nadia *is* / *isn't* disturbing Kate.
3 Jack's phone number is *8693 2210* / *8693 2110* .
4 It's Steve's birthday *tomorrow* / *at the weekend* .
5 Nadia wants to buy a present for *Steve* / *Jack* .
6 She *knows* / *doesn't know* what to buy Steve.

3 Listen and repeat.

1 h<u>e</u>   sh<u>e</u>   m<u>ee</u>t   cr<u>ea</u>m   fourt<u>ee</u>n
2 <u>i</u>f   h<u>i</u>s   f<u>i</u>sh   s<u>i</u>x   ch<u>i</u>cken

Vocabulary Telephone numbers

4 Listen and circle the telephone numbers you hear.

1 721 580 / 712 508
2 299 5043 / 299 5034
3 6619 5832 / 6119 5832

4 2305 5727 / 2350 5727
5 1682 5522 / 1682 2255
6 2867 501 / 2877 501

5 Repeat the telephone numbers.

1 519 2620
2 348 7714

4 9962 5168
5 7342 6600

Get talking Talking on the phone

6 Ask and answer with a partner.

What's your phone number?

It's …

7 Listen and complete the dialogue then practise it with a partner.

Mr Wright 578 312. Hello?
Nadia Hello. Can I [1]........................ to Jack please?
Mr Wright I'm sorry, he isn't [2]........................ Can you call [3]........................ later?
Nadia Yes, OK. Thank you.

8 In pairs, invent similar dialogues changing the names and numbers.

Language Focus

Vocabulary Ordinal numbers

1 Listen and repeat.

1st	the first	9th	the ninth	17th	the seventeenth
2nd	the second	10th	the tenth	18th	the eighteenth
3rd	the third	11th	the eleventh	19th	the nineteenth
4th	the fourth	12th	the twelfth	20th	the twentieth
5th	the fifth	13th	the thirteenth	21st	the twenty-first
6th	the sixth	14th	the fourteenth	30th	the thirtieth
7th	the seventh	15th	the fifteenth		
8th	the eighth	16th	the sixteenth		

Vocabulary Months of the year

2 Listen and repeat.

January and February,
March and April, May and June
Then July is coming soon.

August and September,
October and November,
And finally… December!

3 Read the dates.

Saturday 11th June
Sunday 5th August

Friday 21st December
Tuesday 4th January

Get talking Talking about birthdays

4 Listen and complete.

Sue	When's your ¹............................., Julian?
Julian	On ²............................ 18th.
Sue	Really? My birthday's on December ³............................!
Julian	How ⁴............................ are you?
Sue	I'm ⁵............................ .

> ✲ We write
> **'on May 7th'**.
> We say
> **'on May the seventh'**
> or
> **'on the seventh of May'**.

5 Ask five people when their birthday is then tell the class.

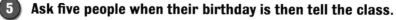

A When's your birthday?

B My birthday's on March 5th.

A Marco's birthday is on March 5th.

Grammar

Present continuous Positive

1 Look at the dialogue on page 100 and complete the table.

I'm	do[1]............ some homework.
He/she/it's	play[2]............ football.
You/we/they're	trying to find something.

✱ Use the Present continuous to talk about actions happening at the moment of speaking.

2 Complete the sentences with *'m*, *'s* or *'re*.

1 **A** Where's Nick?
   B He............ playing football.
2 **A** Let's play table tennis.
   B Sorry. We............ having dinner now.
3 **A** Where are Sandra and Lucy?
   B They............ shopping.
4 **A** Are you OK?
   B Yes, I............ having great fun!
5 **A** Can you help me, please?
   B Sorry, I............ reading a book.
6 **A** Can I talk to Lynn?
   B She isn't at home. She............ riding her bike.

3 Write *am*, *is* or *are*. Use short forms where possible.

1 I .... having dinner.
2 My mother .... watching TV.
3 Our dog .... sleeping.
4 Dad .... washing the car.
5 Granny .... listening to music.
6 They .... playing computer games.
7 .... she doing her homework?
8 .... they enjoying their holiday?

Forming words with *–ing*

> **verb + *ing*:** do – doing, play – playing, enjoy – enjoying
> **e + *ing*:** come – com**ing**, have – hav**ing**, make – mak**ing**
> **double consonants:** stop – sto**pp**ing, sit – si**tt**ing, put – pu**tt**ing

4 Write the *–ing* form of the verbs.

1 watch   *watching*
2 listen   ....
3 swim   ....
4 go   ....
5 read   ....
6 roller skate   ....
7 hit   ....

5 Complete the sentences with the *–ing* form of the verbs. Use short forms.

1 Come round to my place – *we're listening* to music. (listen)
2 Look! The dog .... in the river! (swim)
3 Don't disturb me! I .... a good book. (read)
4 She .... her holiday. (enjoy)
5 They .... a computer game. (play)
6 You .... your homework. (do)

Present continuous Negative

I'm not	enjoying it.
He/she/it isn't	playing computer games.
You/we/they're aren't	winning.

6 **Write the verbs in the negative form.**

1 I'm enjoying my holiday.
   I'm not enjoying my holiday.

2 He's doing his homework.
   ....

3 They're playing tennis.
   ....

4 Nadia's having breakfast.
   ....

5 Steve's sleeping.
   ....

6 We're listening to the teacher.
   ....

7 You're disturbing me.
   ....

8 It's raining.
   ....

Present continuous Questions and short answers

7 **Complete the table with the words below.**

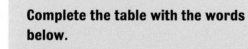

is   am   are   isn't   aren't

Questions	Positive answers	Negative answers
.... I **disturbing** you?	Yes, you **are**.	No, you ....
.... you **listening** to me?	Yes, I **am**.	No, I'**m not**.
.... she **watching** TV?	Yes, she **is**.	No, she ....

8 **Write questions and short answers.**

1 he / watch TV? (✓)
   Is he watching TV ....?
   Yes, he is.

2 they / cook dinner? (✗)
   Are they cooking dinner ....?
   No, they aren't.

3 she / do her homework? (✓)
   ....?
   ....

4 he / have breakfast? (✗)
   ....?
   ....

5 you / play computer games? (✗)
   ....?
   ....

9 **Work with a partner. Look at the pictures for a minute then close your book and try and remember the actions of each person.**

A What's Jacob doing?

B He's … / I can't remember. Give me a clue!

Skills

Listening

11 **1** **Listen to the sounds and guess what the people are doing.**

- [ ] She's playing a computer game.
- [ ] She's sending a text message.
- [ ] They're playing football.
- [ ] She's riding a horse.
- [ ] He's cooking an egg.

- [ ] He's roller skating.
- [ ] He's riding his bike.
- [ ] They're playing the piano.
- [ ] He's looking after his cat.
- [ ] She's skateboarding.

Speaking

2 **Work with a partner. Prepare and practise a telephone conversation. Use your own ideas.**

Tom Hi, Tom speaking.
Sandra Hi, Tom. It's Sandra here.
What are you doing?
Tom I'm playing Super Hero III.
It's great.
Sandra Oh, can I come to your place?
Tom Sure.

1 TV programmes.

I'm watching .... It's great!

I'm watching .... It's fantastic!

2 Music.

I'm listening to .... It's great!

I'm listening to .... It's fantastic!

3 Computer games.

I'm playing .... It's great!

I'm playing .... It's fantastic!

Reading

 3 Read the text and then answer the questions.

Birthdays around the world

"How do you celebrate your birthday?"
"Do you invite lots of your friends?"
"Do you have a party?"

Read what young people around the world do on their special day.

Denmark

In Denmark, they put a flag outside a window to show that someone in that house is having a birthday. They place presents around the birthday child's bed while they are sleeping. When the birthday child wakes up, they are happy when they see their presents.

England

Sometimes, when it's your birthday, your friends give you the 'bumps'. They lift you in the air by your hands and feet and raise you up and down to the floor, one for each year.

Nepal

People make a mixture of rice, yogurt and colouring. Then they make a special mark on the birthday child's forehead. People think this brings good luck.

Vietnam

In Vietnam, people do not celebrate the exact day of their birth. Everyone's birthday is on the same day – New Year's Day. On the first morning of the new year, parents give their children red envelopes. In the envelopes, there is 'Lucky Money'.

In which country ...

1 do they put a coloured mark on the birthday child's face? ....
2 do all children have the same birthday? ....
3 do you wake up to find your birthday presents? ....
4 do boys and girls lift the birthday child in the air? ....
5 do people celebrate their birthday on the first day of the year? ....

A Song 4 U Mr Muddle is never right!

  4 **Listen and sing.**

Where is everybody?
Well... John is playing computer games
and Suzie's riding her horse.
Bob is looking after his cat, yeah,
and Lucy's cooking some sauce.

Ah, I see ...

John is playing his cat, right?
And Suzie's cooking her horse.
Bob's looking after his computer game,
and Lucy's riding some sauce.

Chorus
Mr Muddle, he's always
in trouble.
Mr Muddle, Mr Muddle,
he's never right.

Oh, sorry ...

John is cooking computer games,
and Suzie's playing her horse.
Bob is riding his cat, I think?
And who's looking after the sauce?

Mr Muddle, he's always
in trouble.
Mr Muddle, Mr Muddle,
he's always wrong.

Chorus

He's always wrong!

Writing for your Portfolio

5 **Read and write a postcard.**

Dear Maria,
I'm sitting in a café and I'm drinking hot chocolate.
It's nice and warm in here. It's very cold outside. It's snowing.
Jack's snowboarding and Mum and Dad are skiing. We're having fun.
See you soon. Robert

The Carnival of the Animals

Key words

concert	composer	performer	piece of music
symphony	compose	track	imagine

1 Read this text about a famous composer and performer.

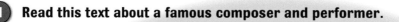

Camille Saint-Saëns

Paris, 1838: Camille Saint-Saëns is three years old. He can already read and write and has piano lessons. Soon, he also starts composing his own music. When Camille is 10, he gives his first concerts as a singer. He sings Bach, Beethoven and Mozart. When he is sixteen, he writes his first symphony.

Camille Saint-Saëns becomes famous. He writes over three hundred pieces of music, among them 13 operas. He becomes the first composer to write music for the cinema.

Saint-Saëns travels a lot. He goes around Europe, North Africa, and South America. Camille Saint-Saëns dies on December 16, 1921 in Algiers.

One of Camille Saint-Saëns most famous works is *The Carnival of the Animals*. Many people find it easy to listen to the music and imagine the animals.

13 **2** Listen and number the pictures in the correct order.

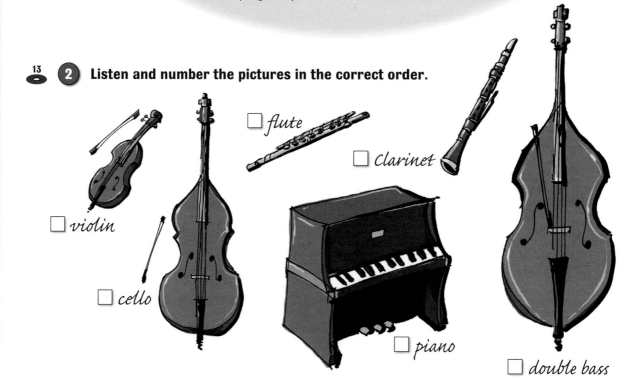

☐ *flute*

☐ *Clarinet*

☐ *violin*

☐ *cello*

☐ *piano*

☐ *double bass*

The Carnival of the Animals

 3a Look at the photos of the animals/fish. Which instruments do you think represent each one?

The Cuckoo

The Swan

The Aquarium

The Elephant

Hens and Cockerels

 14 3b Now listen to the tracks. Then answer the following questions in your notebook.

1 What instrument(s) is / are playing?	I can hear …
2 What animal / track is it?	I think it's …
3 What do you imagine?	I imagine … / I can see …
4 Do you like it? Why?	Yes, I like it because …
	No, I don't like it because …

15 3c Listen to the tracks again. Then work with a partner. Compare your answers. Do you agree?

Mini-project

4 Choose a new animal to add to *The Carnival of the Animals*. Think of adjectives that describe this animal *(big, small, dangerous, friendly)*.

5 Now think about how to describe this animal through music. What instrument 'plays' your animal? How does this animal make you feel?

6 Work in groups of four. Compare your different animals. Which is your favourite animal? When you decide, draw a picture of this animal and write a short description of the music.

In this unit

You learn
- articles
- present simple vs. present continuous
- words for computers
- words for free-time activities

and then you can
- make invitations
- talk about your free time

16

1 **Listen and read.**

(On the phone)

Nadia Hi, Jack. What are you doing right now?

Jack I'm feeding my hamster and I'm cleaning its cage.

Nadia Can you come over to my place?

Jack Why? What's going on?

Nadia Steve and I are playing a computer game but we've got a problem with the computer.

Jack OK, give me ten minutes.

(Ten minutes later)

Steve Is it a virus?

Jack I don't think so. Nadia, how often do you run an anti-virus program?

Nadia Every day.

Jack I think there's something wrong with the hard disk. Take it to the computer shop tomorrow.

Nadia OK. Well, now I've got more time for reading.

Steve Do you like reading?

Nadia Yes, I do. What about you?

Steve Well, I only read the TV guide.

2 Match the two parts of the sentences.

1 Jack's feeding
2 Nadia and Steve are playing
3 Nadia runs an anti-virus
4 Jack thinks there is
5 Nadia likes
6 Steve only reads

a a computer game.
b something wrong with the hard disk.
c his hamster.
d the TV guide.
e program every day.
f reading.

Get talking Making invitations

  3 Listen and repeat.

Tom Would you like to meet at the youth club?
Kate Sure. Let's meet there in half an hour.

Daisy Do you want to play tennis with me?
Dean Sorry, I can't.

Lucy Would you like to come to the football game with me?
Jack I'd love to.

4 Work with a partner. Use the pictures to invent dialogues.

Language Focus

burn
check
click
~~create~~
run
save
send
surf

Vocabulary Computers

1 **Complete the expressions with the verbs on the left.**

1 to _create_ a backup of your files
2 to .... your hard disk for viruses
3 to .... an email to a friend
4 to .... your files on your hard disk

5 to .... a program
6 to .... with a mouse
7 to .... the Internet
8 to .... a CD

Vocabulary Free time activities

18 **2** **Listen and write the expressions under the pictures.**

....

....

....

....

....

....

....

....

....

....

....

....

Get talking Talking about your free time

3 **Ask and answer with a partner.**

What do you do in your free time?
How often do you do it?
How much time do you spend on it?
Who do you do it with?

an hour a day / two hours a week

once a month / every day

my friend(s) / my brother / on my own

Grammar

Articles

1 **Look at the dialogue on page 110 and complete the examples.**

I only read [1].......... TV guide.
Steve and I are playing [2]..........
computer game.
How often do you run [3].......... anti-virus
program?
There's something wrong with [4]..........
hard disc.

✱ The indefinite articles are *a* and *an*.
  A is used before nouns that begin
  with a consonant.
  An is used before nouns that begin
  with a vowel sound.

✱ The definite article is *the*.

2 **Reorder the words and write complete sentences.**

1 cat / I've / a / got
  I've got a cat.

2 dogs / are / Where / the
  ....

3 father / policeman / My / is / a
  ....

4 house / in / live / a / We / small
  ....

5 apple / you / Would / an / like
  ....

6 a / you / Have / bike / got
  ....

7 near / lives / airport / an / He
  ....

8 the / of / capital / is / London / England
  ....

9 got / American / We've / car / an
  ....

10 river / Where / the / Nile / is
  ....

3 **Complete the sentences with *a, an* or *the*.**

1 He drives ...*an*.... old car.
2 .... hospital in our town is very good.
3 It's .... really good film.
4 Who is .... actor in that film?
5 Where are .... sandwiches?
6 That's .... lovely dog.
7 I've got .... orange bike.
8 He's .... President of the USA.
9 They live in .... big city.
10 There's .... computer on my desk.

Sounds right *The*

4 **Listen and repeat.**

19

1 I want the cheese sandwich not the egg
  sandwich.
2 I live in the old house not the new house.
3 I want to go to the hospital not the airport.
4 She drives the Audi not the Fiat.

Sounds right /w/

5 **A chant. Listen and repeat.**

20

We can hang out **w**ith friends,
We can **w**atch TV,
We can **w**alk, **w**e can talk –
Have a **w**eekend with me!

Present simple vs. present continuous

What **are you** do**ing** right now?
I'm feed**ing** my hamster.
Steve and I **are** play**ing** computer games.

How often **do** you **run** an anti-virus program?
Does she like reading?
I only **read** about TV programmes.

 6 **Study the examples and complete the rules with the Present simple or Present continuous.**

* To talk about habit, routines and general information, we use the
  1 ....

* To talk about what's happening at the moment of speaking we use the
  2 ....

* We always use the verb *'to be'* in the Present 3 ....

* We use *do* and *does* to make questions in the Present 4 ....

* We use *don't* and *doesn't* to make negative sentences in the Present
  5 ....

* We add an *–s* to the third person in the Present 6 ....

7 **Match the questions and answers.**

1 What are you watching?
2 What kind of programmes do you watch?
3 Where are you going?
4 Where does she live?
5 Who are you talking to?
6 How often do you talk to Bob?

a I like programmes about animals.
b To my granny's house.
c Every day.
d A programme about crocodiles.
e A friend from school.
f 32, Highgrove Court.

8 **Circle the correct form of the verb.**

1 Can you phone me in five minutes?
  I *watch / am watching* TV at the moment.
2 I *live / am living* at 123, Charles Street.
3 **A** Where's Paul?
  B He's in the kitchen. He *cooks / is cooking* dinner.
4 We *play / are playing* tennis every Friday.
5 She *reads / is reading* three books a week.

9 **Complete the sentences with the Present simple or the Present continuous form of the verbs.**

1 They always .... their grandparents in the holidays. (visit)
2 I really .... cooking. (like)
3 He can't speak on the phone because he .... a shower. (have)
4 Look at that man. He .... a horse. (ride)
5 We sometimes .... to the cinema on a Sunday. (go)
6 I .... about three DVDs a week. (watch)

10 **Complete the dialogue with the Present simple or the Present continuous form of the verbs.**

Chris Where 1 .... you ....?? (go)
Jack I 2 .... my computer to the shop. (take)
Chris What 3 .... the problem with it? (be)
Jack It 4 .... a virus on the hard disk. (have got)
Chris Don't you know how to fix it?
Jack I 5 .... anything about computers. (not know)
Chris 6 .... you .... me to have a look? (want)
Jack If you're not busy.
Chris Sure, I 7 .... anything. (not do)

 11 **Listen and check then practise the dialogue with a partner.**

21

Skills

Listening and speaking

22 **1** Listen to the interview and tick the answer you hear.

	What is the pet?	What colour is it?	Where does it sleep?	How often do they feed it?	How much time a day do they spend with it?
Megan	a cat ☐ a hamster ☐ a dog ☐	black and white ☐ black and grey ☐ black, white and brown ☐	in Megan's room ☐ in the bathroom ☐ in the living room ☐	once a day ☐ twice a day ☐ three times a day ☐	15 minutes ☐ 50 minutes ☐ 90 minutes ☐
David	a cat ☐ a hamster ☐ a dog ☐	black ☐ brown ☐ brown and white ☐	in the hall ☐ in David's room ☐ in the living room ☐	once a day ☐ twice a day ☐ three times a day ☐	15 minutes ☐ 50 minutes ☐ 90 minutes ☐

23 **2** Listen to the interview again and complete the sentences.

1 Megan doesn't often ....
2 When Megan does her homework her cat ....
3 David's sister doesn't ....

3 Interview three students in your class. If you haven't got a pet, invent one.

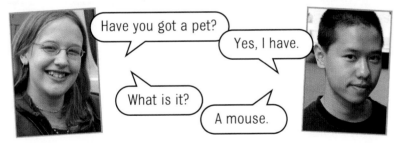

Have you got a pet?
Yes, I have.
What is it?
A mouse.

Names of classmates	Have you got a pet?	What is it?	What colour is it?	Where does it sleep?	How often do you feed it?	How much time a day do you spend with it?

4 Tell the class about your interviews.

Nathalie has got a ... It's ... It sleeps ...
She feeds it ... She spends ... minutes a day with it.

Reading

5 **Read the text and circle T (True) or F (False).**

so STRANGE! People have got strange hobbies!

Mr and Mrs Ball live in Oxford. They collect garden gnomes. They've got 225 in their garden! The gnomes are all different colours and come from different countries.

Today, Mr and Mrs Ball are preparing a big garden party for their gnomes. They are putting lanterns on the trees and decorating the garden with colourful balloons. 'We're writing

225 invitations and we are putting up little tables and chairs for the gnomes, 'Mrs Ball says. 'It's a lot of work, but it's fun!'

1   There are a lot of gnomes in Mr and Mrs Ball's garden. T / F
2   The gnomes are all from the UK. T / F
3   The gnomes are not very colourful. T / F
4   Mr and Mrs Ball are having a party. T / F

A song 4 U Super-sonic surfer

24 6 **Listen and sing the song.**

Every day
When I finish school
My friends always say
"Why are you so cool?"
"Is it because you
like dancing?
Or play the guitar?
Is it because you
like swimming
Or can run very far?"

Chorus
And I say ...
"I'm a super-sonic surfer
And I surf all day
I surf the Net
So I can get
New games to play.

I'm a super-sonic surfer
And I surf all night
I surf the Net
So I can get
My homework right!"

Every weekend
When I get up late
My sister always
asks me
"Why are you so great?"
"Is it because you play
computer games,
And basketball too?
Oh why, oh why can't I be
As great as you?!"

Chorus

"I'm a super-sonic surfer
And I surf all day
I surf the Net
So I can get
New games to play."

MORE fun with Fido

Yuk!

That's better!

Check your progress Units 9 and 10

1 **Complete the names of the months**

1 J _ n _ a _ y
2 F _ b _ _ a _ y
3 M _ r _ h
4 _ p _ i _
5 _ a _
6 J _ n _

7 J _ _ _
8 _ ug _ s _
9 S _ _ _ em _ _ r
10 _ ct _ _ er
11 N _ v _ _ b _ _
12 _ e _ e _ _e _

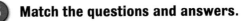 12

2 **Write answers using the correct form of the verb.**

1 What's John doing this morning?
   He .... (read) the new Harry Potter book.
2 Where does your penfriend live?
   She .... (live) in Sweden.
3 Why can't we listen to music?
   Because my sister .... (sleep)!
4 Where is Grace this morning?
   She .... (play) tennis with her mum.
5 Do you want to watch the news with me?
   I can't. I .... (cook) dinner.
6 Do your parents like going to the cinema?
   Yes, they .... (go) once a week.

6

3 **Rewrite the sentences using the negative form.**

1 I'm having breakfast.

   ....

2 They're enjoying their holiday.

   ....

3 We go to France every summer.

   ....

4 He knows my sister very well.

   ....

5 She's listening to the new CD by *Razorlight*.

   ....

10

4 **Circle the correct article.**

1 My brother is *a / an / the* doctor.
2 *A / An / The* centre of town is very busy.
3 My teacher has got *a / an / the* new car.
4 Would you like *a / an / the* orange juice?

5 Who is *a / an / the* singer that wears sunglasses?
6 There's *a / an / the* old hospital next to my school.

6

5 **Match the questions and answers.**

1 Are you watching MTV?
2 How often do you watch TV?
3 Do you like computer games?
4 Are your parents going on holiday?
5 Is it raining?
6 When does school start?

a Every day.
b At half past eight.
c Yes, they are.
d No, I'm listening to music.
e No, I don't.
f Yes, it is.

6

6 **Answer the questions.**

1 What sports do you do?

   ....

2 How often do you go to the cinema?

   ....

3 When's your birthday?

   ....

4 What do you do in your free time?

   ....

5 Have you got a pet?

   ....

10

TOTAL 50

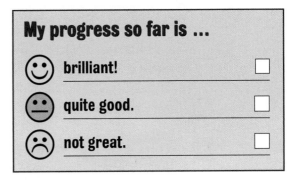

My progress so far is ...

☺ **brilliant!** ☐

😐 **quite good.** ☐

☹ **not great.** ☐

Spend spend spend

1 **Read the text about British teenagers and circle T (True) or F (False).**

Teenagers in Britain aged 10 to 14 earn about £775 a year. They do household chores and newspaper rounds. They also get pocket money from their parents. They spend their pocket money on trendy clothes, CDs, DVDs, beauty products, soft drinks, sweets and mobile phones. Young people spend on average £26 a year on ringtones, ring-back tones and downloading songs.

FACT FILE

Teenagers (10–14 year olds) in Europe earn in a year ...

Britain £775	Germany £438
Sweden £697	Italy £341
Netherlands £575	Spain £310
France £442	

Source: Datamonitor

1 Some teenagers in Britain earn money from part-time jobs. T / F
2 Their parents don't give them any money. T / F
3 They don't spend their money on clothes. T / F
4 They like buying CDs and DVDs. T / F
5 They don't spend any money on music for their mobile phones. T / F

25 **2** **Listen and complete the table with information about Lucy.**

	LUCY	JAMES	....	....
How much pocket money do you get a week?				
Have you got a part-time job?				
How much money do you spend a week?				
What do you spend your money on?				

3 **Read the paragraph and complete the table with information about James.**

Hi, my name's James. I'm thirteen years old. I get £5 a week pocket money from my parents. I spend that money on my mobile phone and sweets. I've also got a part-time job. I earn £15 a week. I don't spend any of that money. I save it. I want to buy an MP3 player.

4 **Interview two friends and complete the table with information about them.**

5 **Over 2 U!** **Write a paragraph about what you spend your money on.**

MORE! And now you can watch *Kids in the UK!*

Poems

I haven't got a pet

I've got a father and a mother,
And a very smelly brother,
A grandma and a grandpa:
But I haven't got a pet.
I've got an auntie and an uncle,
Little sisters by the dozen,
Ninety-seven second cousins:
But I haven't got a pet.
Except ....
I have got a slug
Which I keep under the rug.
Don't tell Mum!

Cross Country

Nine o'clock on the dot.
Right, you miserable lot.
Silence! Do up your
running shoes,
I have a muddy field
waiting for you.

There's the door. Out you go.
Yes I know there's a storm.
That's why I'm staying here
where it's nice and warm.

What's this? A note?
You've broken your leg?
I'm not falling for this.
You can hop instead.

For **MORE!** Go to www.cambridge.org/elt/more and do a quiz on these poems.

In this unit

You learn
- past simple of *be*
- past time expressions
- words for furniture

and then you can
- ask where people were
- say where things are

26 **1** **Listen and read.**

Nadia Adam, were you in my bedroom yesterday evening?

Adam No, I wasn't. Why?

Nadia Somebody was in there and I can't find my diary now. Where were you?

Adam Well, I wasn't in there. I was here in the living room. There was a football match on TV.

Nadia When was that?

Adam From 8 to 10 pm.

Nadia I don't believe you! I was in here at 9.30 and you weren't here.

Adam I was. Dad and I were in here all the time.

Nadia Mum!

Mum What is it?

Nadia I can't find my diary. I think Adam was in my room.

Adam No, I wasn't.

Mum Your diary? It's in the kitchen – on the fridge behind the basket. Remember? You were in there yesterday evening – with your diary.

Nadia Was I? Oh yes, I remember. Sorry, Adam. Mum, is my MP3 player in there too?

Adam Your MP3 player? Err, um…

Nadia What?

Adam The match was boring so…

Nadia Adam!

2 **Circle T (True) or F (False) for the sentences below.**

1 Nadia can't find her diary. T / F
2 Adam was in the living room from 8 to 9.30. T / F
3 Nadia was in the living room at 10 o'clock, too. T / F
4 Mum has got the diary. T / F
5 The diary wasn't in the kitchen. T / F
6 Nadia was in the kitchen yesterday evening. T / F

Get talking Asking where people were

27 **3** **Listen and repeat.**

A Where was Nadia yesterday evening?   **A** Where were Mum and Dad at 9.30?
B She was in the kitchen.   **B** They were in the dining room.

4 **Ask and answer questions.**

A Where was / were… at 4pm?

B He / She was / They were at the…

1 Paul – 4 pm
   shopping centre

2 Debbie – 3 pm
   park

3 Sue and John – 8 pm
   cinema

4 Dawn – 9 am
   bus stop

5 Kevin – 5 pm
   sports centre

6 Tim and Sharon – 6 pm
   train station

Sounds right

I was hot!

28 **5** **Listen and repeat.**

He was happy.	I wasn't happy.	Was he happy?
I was hot.	I was sad.	Yes, he was.
She was happy.	They were happy.	Were you happy?
I was not.	I was mad.	No, because…

Language Focus

Vocabulary Furniture

 1 Look at the picture. Write the number next to the correct word. Then listen and check.

`4` wardrobe
☐ fridge
☐ sink
☐ radiator
☐ bed
☐ cooker
☐ cupboard
☐ sofa
☐ table
☐ armchair
☐ carpet
☐ curtain
☐ chair
☐ bedside table
☐ rug
☐ lamp

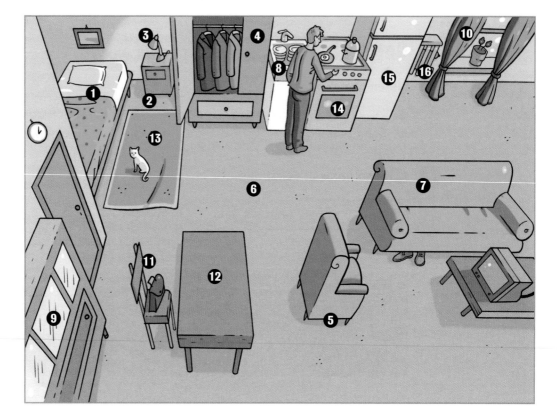

Get talking Saying where things are

2 Look at the picture. Complete the sentences with the words on the left.

on
between
above
in front of
under
in
next to
behind

1 There are some plates .... the sink.
2 There is a cat .... the rug.
3 There is a pair of shoes .... the sofa.
4 There are some flowers .... the curtains.
5 There is a man .... the cooker.
6 There is a door .... the cupboard.
7 There is a blue coat .... a red and a green coat in the wardrobe.
8 There is a picture .... the bed.

3 Work with a partner. Student A closes his eyes. Student B asks questions about the classroom. Change roles.

A Is there a clock above the board?

B Yes, there is. / No, there isn't.

Grammar

Past simple of *be* Positive and negative

1 **Look at the sentences below.**

I **was** in the living room.
Nadia and Adam **were** at home.

There **wasn't** a football match on TV.
You **weren't** there.

Now complete the table.

Positive	Negative
I ¹...................... in the living room.	I wasn't in the kitchen. (was not)
You were at home.	You weren't with him. (were not)
He was in his bedroom.	He ⁵...................... with us. (was not)
She ²...................... with me.	She wasn't in her bedroom. (was not)
It was on the fridge.	It ⁶...................... in your bedroom. (was not)
We were in the living room.	We weren't at home. (were not)
You ³...................... in the bedroom.	You ⁷...................... at home. (were not)
They ⁴...................... in the kitchen.	They ⁸...................... alone. (were not)

2 **Circle the correct form of *be* in each sentence.**

1 At four o'clock I *was / were* in my room, not in the living room.
2 They *wasn't / weren't* at home, they *was / were* in the park.
3 It *was / were* a great match and you *was / were* fantastic. Congratulations!
4 She *wasn't / weren't* at home.
5 The bananas *was / were* in the fridge, not on the table.
6 We *wasn't / weren't* at home yesterday evening. We *was / were* at the cinema.

3 **Complete the sentences with *was* or *were*.**

1 I .... at school from 8 to 3 yesterday.
2 Jane and Nick .... at the shopping centre this morning.
3 You .... not at home.
4 She .... my sister's best friend.
5 Our teacher .... angry.
6 We .... late for school this morning.

4 **Make the sentences negative.**

1 I was at home on Sunday.
   I wasn't at home on Sunday.
2 They were very hungry last night.
   ....
3 She was at the supermarket from 8 to 10.
   ....
4 You were very friendly to me.
   ....
5 My books were on my desk.
   ....

They were not alone!

Past simple of *be* Questions and short answers

 Look at the sentences below.

Were you in my bedroom? No, I **wasn't**.   **Was** the football game on TV yesterday? Yes, it **was**.

Now complete the table.

Questions	Short answers	
	Positive	Negative
Was I late?	Yes, I was.	No, I wasn't.
Were you in my room?	Yes, you [1]................. .	No, you weren't.
Was he in my room?	Yes, he was.	No, he [6]................. .
Was she in my room?	Yes, she [2]................. .	No, she [7]................. .
Was it cold?	Yes, it [3]................. .	No, it [8]................. .
Were we late?	Yes, we were.	No, we weren't.
Were you late?	Yes, you [4]................. .	No, you [9]................. .
Were they late?	Yes, they [5]................. .	No, they [10]................. .

 Complete the questions and the short answers.

1 **A** Were you at the cinema?
  B Yes, *I was.*..........

2 **A** .... she at the supermarket?
  B No, ...

3 **A** .... your friends on holiday?
  B No, ...

4 **A** .... we right?
  B Yes, ...

5 **A** .... I wrong?
  B No, ...

6 **A** .... Thomas with you?
  B Yes, ...

Past time expressions

You were there **yesterday evening**.
Where were you **at 5 o'clock**?
Where were you **from 6 to 9**?
Last Sunday I was at a football game.
I was not at home **yesterday**.

 Translate these expressions.

1 yesterday   ....
2 yesterday evening   ....
3 at 5 o'clock   ....
4 from 7 to 9   ....
5 last Friday   ....
6 last Friday at
   9 o'clock   ....

8 **Work with a partner. Ask questions to find out where your partner was at the times below.**

Where were you...

yesterday at 4 pm?
yesterday at midnight?
last Friday at 5 pm?
last Friday at 12 am?
last Saturday at 6 pm?
last Saturday at 10 pm?
last Sunday at 10 am?

I was ...

at home.
in the park.
at school.
at the cinema.
in my bedroom.
at a friend's place.
at a football game.

Skills

Reading and listening

 1 **Read the beginning of the story.**

Robbery at Hanbury Hall

Hanbury Hall is the home of Lord and Lady Brown. Last night there was a robbery at Hanbury Hall. This morning the clock in the library is missing! It was a very valuable clock. There were diamonds in the back!

Lady Brown is talking to Inspector Clue. He's a policeman from Scotland Yard. He wants to find the robber.

30 **2** **Listen to Lady Brown and Inspector Clue and write these jobs under the correct people.**

cook   maid   butler

Lord and Lady Brown

Henry Brown, their son

Miss Green

Mrs Black

Mr White

31 **3** Read and listen. Write which people were in these rooms last night.

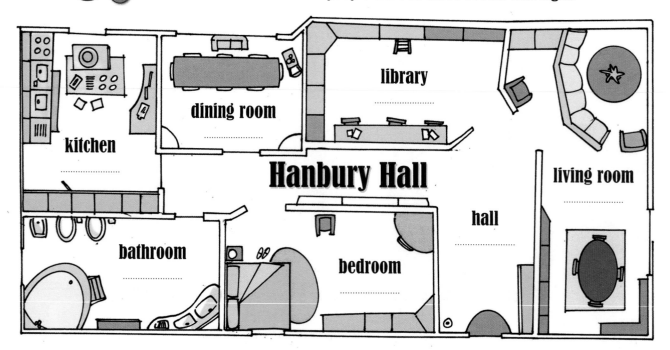

library

dining room

kitchen

Hanbury Hall

living room

bathroom

hall

bedroom

Inspector	Where were you at 9 pm, Lady Brown?
Lady Brown	I was with my husband. We were in the living room.
Inspector	Was your son Henry with you?
Lady Brown	No, he wasn't. He was in his bedroom, I think.

Inspector	Were your parents with you last night at 9 pm?
Henry Brown	No, they weren't. They were in the library, I think.
Inspector	You weren't in the library?
Henry Brown	No, I was in my bedroom. I was very tired.

Inspector	Mrs Black, where were you at 9 pm?
Mrs Black	I was in the kitchen all evening.
Inspector	All evening?
Mrs Black	Yes, I always prepare breakfast in the evening.

Inspector	Where were you at 9 pm last night, Mr White?
Mr White	I was in the hall.
Inspector	Were you alone?
Mr White	No, I was with Miss Green.

---

32 **4** Who is not telling the truth? Look at the picture of the library on page 125.
Find something belonging to the robber. Then listen and check your answer.

Speaking

5 Look at the picture and talk about the people. Use the words on the left.

sad
happy
hungry
cold
scared
angry

At 5 o'clock Brian was in the kitchen. He was hungry.
At ... Sally and Fred were ... . They were ...

Writing for your Portfolio

6 Write a short text about your day yesterday.

A busy day

Yesterday was very busy. At 7 am I was in the kitchen. I was hungry and breakfast was good. From 8 am to 3 pm I was at school. School was OK but I was tired. I was in the gym at 4 pm and, at 5 pm, I was in the swimming pool. I was at home at 6 pm, and I was hungry again. At 9 pm I was in bed.

Money

Key words

cash	paper money (banknotes)
coins	plastic money
silver	currency converter
gold	bank card
salary	credit card

1a Do the quiz. Tick the correct country.

1	The pound (£) is the money in	☐ India	☐ Britain	☐ the USA	☐ Ireland
2	The euro (€) is the money in	☐ Ireland	☐ Britain	☐ Japan	☐ Brazil
3	The real (R$) is the money in	☐ the USA	☐ China	☐ Japan	☐ Brazil
4	The dollar ($) is the money in	☐ Britain	☐ China	☐ Brazil	☐ the USA
5	The yen (¥) is the money in	☐ China	☐ Japan	☐ Brazil	☐ India

33

1b Now listen and check.

2 What is money?

When most people think of money, they think of it as a thing we can use to buy or pay for something. But in the past, money was also something used in traditional and religious ceremonies, such as weddings. We often think of money as coins or notes (cash) but in the past people used many different things as 'money'.

Many people in the world today keep their money in banks. What most people don't know is that banks are older than money. There were banks in Ancient Mesopotamia and Ancient Egypt.

Did you know?

3 Read the texts about money.

Ancient Mesopotamia:	**Turkey 600 BC:**	**China 800 AD:**
The first banks. Rich families have rooms in their palaces where people can keep food and things to sell. Money does not exist.	People in Turkey make the first coins from gold and silver (the Lydian coin).	People make the first paper money.

Mini-project

4 **Find a currency converter on the Internet. How much are these in your money?**

£1 (one British pound) = ... $1 (one US dollar) = ...

5 **Look at these prices from the past. Use a calculator to find out how much these things cost in the currency of your country today.**

Example: You live in Singapore. The currency in Singapore is the Singapore dollar (SGD). £1.00 = 3.03 SGD
The first mobile costs £1,864.   In today's money: 5588.97 SGD

	England – 1984:	**Prices** (in today's money):
	The first mobile phones costs £1,864.	....
	A computer costs about £4,000.	....
	A video recorder costs about £525.	....

	USA – 1900:	**Prices** (in today's money):
	A worker's salary per year is about $550	....
	A teacher's income per year is about $2.000	....
	The rent for a flat (2–3 rooms) was $6 per month	....

6 **Find out about prices in the past in your country. Ask a parent, aunt or uncle, or grandparent the following questions.**

- How much was their first flat/house?
- How much was their first car?
- How much was their first television?
- How much was their first salary?

Europe around 1500:
In this picture you can see how people are making coins in the year 1500.

Sweden around 1660:
The Bank of Sweden prints the first paper money in Europe.

Southeast Asia and Africa before 1900:
People use cowry shells for money.

Today:
More and more people do not use banknotes or coins. They use plastic money (bank cards and credit cards).

⊕ Money Bank   platinum
0000 1234 5678 9000
VALID 09/09 – 09/09
MR FIRST NAME SURNAME

34 **1** **Listen and read.**

Nadia	Hi, Steve. I'm going to the record shop after school. Do you want to come?
Steve	No, thanks.
Nadia	What's the matter? Are you alright?
Steve	Yeah, I'm OK.
Nadia	No, you're not. What's the problem?
Steve	Oh, OK. It's football.
Nadia	Football. Again. What now?
Steve	Well I played for the school team against King George High school.
Nadia	When? This morning?
Steve	Yes. The game finished about an hour ago.
Nadia	What was the score?
Steve	4–3 to them. We really wanted to win.
Nadia	Oh dear. But it's not the end of the world.
Steve	It is. I scored a goal.
Nadia	You scored a goal. That's great.
Steve	No, it's not. I scored in the wrong goal. I scored the winning goal for them.

Circle T (True) or F (False) for the sentences below.

1 Nadia's got a problem. T / F
2 Steve is happy. T / F
3 Steve played football yesterday. T / F
4 Steve goes to King George High school. T / F
5 The score was 4–3 to King George High school. T / F
6 Steve scored a goal for his team. T / F

Get talking Saying when you were somewhere

3 **Look at the pictures and say where Enrique was.**

The time is 11 am.
The date is
22nd March 2008.

10:50 am 22/03/2008

Enrique was on a bus 10 minutes ago.

08:00 am 22/03/2007

03:00 am 22/03/2008

20/03/2008

22/09/2007

08:00 am 22/03/2007

4 **Ask and answer questions with your partner.**

10 minutes   2 hours   8 hours
2 days   1 week   1 year

A Where were you 10 minutes ago?
B I was here with you!

Language Focus

Vocabulary Shops

1 Write the correct numbers for the shops.

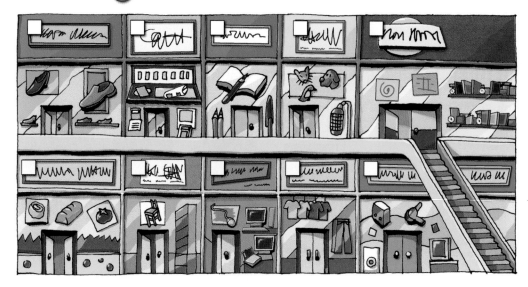

1 electronics shop
2 pet shop
3 shoe shop
4 stationer's
5 record shop
6 computer shop
7 newsagent's
8 clothes shop
9 furniture shop
10 grocer's

2 Where can you buy these things? Write the name of the shop then add two more things to each list.

1 pet shop .... : dogs, cats, ... , ...
2 .... : pen, ruler, ... , ...
3 .... : newspaper, magazine, ... , ...
4 .... : a mouse, a hard-disk, ... , ...
5 .... : jacket, socks, ... , ...
6 .... : trainers, boots, ... , ...
7 .... : CDs, music DVDs, ... , ...
8 .... : cherries, spinach, ... , ...
9 .... : TV, stereo, ... , ...
10 .... : cupboard, wardrobe, ... , ...

Get talking Talking about shopping

35 **3** Listen and complete.

Ali   I need to buy [1]..................... .

Kiki   OK, we need to go to a [2]..................... .

Ali   [3]..................... is the nearest one.

Kiki   There's one in [4]..................... Street.

4 Work with a partner. Choose items from the list in Exercise 2 and talk about shops in your town.

Grammar

Past simple Positive

1 **Complete the examples from the dialogue with the words in the box.**

> scored played finished wanted

1 I .... for the school team.
2 The game .... about an hour ago.
3 We really .... to win.
4 I .... a goal.

2 **Complete the rule.**

✱ To use regular verbs in the past tense we add -¹........... to the end of the verb. If the verb ends in -*e*, then we just add -²...........

3 **Write the Past simple forms of these verbs.**

walk	....	look	....
wait	....	open	....
love	....	like	....
relax	....	hate	....
watch	....	live	....
listen	....	play	....
surf	....	borrow	....
close	....	wiggle	....
touch	....	happen	....
climb	....	dance	....
talk	....	phone	....

Jennifer phoned for help.

Sounds right /t/ /d/ /ɪd/

4 **Listen and repeat.**

36

/t/
1 She jumped in the river.
2 My dog chased a cat.
3 We watched a film.

/d/
4 She phoned at 5 o'clock.
5 He arrived on Monday.
6 We rescued the dog.

/ɪd/
7 I waited for an hour.
8 They shouted at me.
9 She wanted an ice cream.

5 **Use the verbs from Exercise 4 to complete the story.**

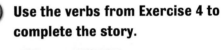

1 There was a boy in the river.
2 He .... 'Help!'

3 I .... into the river.
4 I .... the boy.

6 **Complete each sentence with the Past simple form of the verb.**

1 It .... a sunny day. (be)
2 Helen .... to the park. (walk)
3 In the park she .... her friend Manju. (phone)
4 Helen .... for 15 minutes and Manju .... (wait / arrive)
5 The girls .... to the river. (walk)
6 There .... two boys there. (be)
7 Suddenly the big boy .... the small boy into the river. (push)
8 Helen .... into the river. (jump)
9 Helen .... the boy. (rescue)
10 Manju .... the ambulance and the police. (call)
11 The paramedics and police .... (arrive)
12 They .... the girls. (interview)

7 **Match the sentences from Exercise 6 with the pictures.**

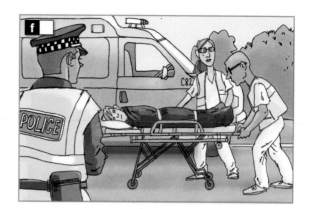

Skills

Reading

1 Read the stories and match them to the pictures.

THE CUP-HOLDER

Mr Custer was happy. On his desk was a new computer. It was a really good one with a DVD and a great flatscreen. After two weeks he phoned the computer shop. "I like my new computer very much," he said, "but I've got a big problem with it."

"What is it?" the shop assistant asked.

"It's the cup-holder," said Mr Custer.

"I don't understand," the man at the shop said. "What cup-holder?"

"The cup-holder at the front of the computer doesn't work. It goes in and spills my coffee."

The cup-holder was the DVD drive.

MODERN ART

Mrs Caroline Smith started work as a cleaning lady in the Museum of Modern Art. The director asked her to clean a room on the first floor. Two hours' later Mrs Smith finished and asked what to do next. The director checked her work. He returned with a look of horror on his face.

The room was certainly clean. The floor and the windows were clean. But he also noticed that part of a modern sculpture was missing. The sculpture was an old jacket over a computer screen. On the jacket there were two roses. But the jacket and the roses weren't there. "Where's the jacket with the roses?" the director asked Mrs Smith. "Oh, that old thing!" she answered. "I cleaned it away! And the roses too!" The sculpture was worth £50,000!

2 Read again and match the sentence halves.

1 Mr Custer liked
2 Mr Custer phoned
3 The shop assistant asked
4 Mr Custer used
5 Mrs Smith worked
6 The museum director was
7 Mrs Smith decided
8 Mrs Smith cleaned away

a Mr Custer about his problem.
b in a museum.
c not happy with Mrs Smith.
d the sculpture.
e the computer shop.
f his computer.
g the sculpture was rubbish.
h the DVD drive for a cup holder.

Listening

37 **3** **Listen to the story and correct the mistakes.**

1 Mrs Browning was at the airport to meet her brother.
2 The plane arrived from Dallas.
3 The man was in a black coat.
4 The man was happy to see Mrs Browning.
5 They pushed the man into a taxi.
6 The man wanted to go to Italy.

A song 4 U A summer holiday

38 **4** **Complete the song with the words then listen, check and sing.**

meet
read
cry
stay
join
watch

(It's a summer, a summer holiday!) (x 2)

No homework for six weeks or so,
Fun and laughter all day long. (*all day long*)
Don't ¹................. my friends, it's time to go.
Cheer up, join in, what's wrong?
(What's wrong?)

Chorus (x 2)
It's a summer, a summer holiday.
Come, wipe your tears, your tears away.
It's a summer, a summer holiday!
A summer holiday!

³................. books and ⁴................. a DVD,
⁵................. your friends and ⁶................. up late.
(Stay up late)
In summer, you, you are free.
Hey, isn't this just great? *(Isn't this just great?)*

Chorus (x 4)

Check your progress Units 11 and 12

1 **Complete the names of the furniture.**

1 w _ r _ _ _ b _   4 b _ _
2 s _ _ k   5 c _ _ _ _ r
3 c _ p _ _ _ _ d   6 a _ _ _ h _ _ r
                                              ☐ 6

2 **Complete the shop names.**

1 r _ _ _ _ _ _   s _ _ _
2 s _ _ _   s _ _ _
3 n _ _ _ _ _ _ _ _ _
4 e _ _ _ _ _ _ _ _ _   s _ _ _
5 c _ _ _ _ _ _   s _ _ _
6 s _ _ _ _ _ _ _ _
7 g _ _ _ _ _ _
8 p _ _   s _ _ _
9 f _ _ _ _ _ _ _   s _ _ _
10 c _ _ _ _ _ _ _   s _ _ _
                                              ☐ 10

3 **Complete the dialogue with the Past simple of *to be*.**

A Where ¹.................. you yesterday afternoon?
B I ².................. at the cinema.
A ³.................. the film good?
B No, it ⁴.................. . It ⁵.................. rubbish!
                                              ☐ 5

4 **Complete the dialogue with the Past simple of the verbs.**

A I ¹.................. (see) a great film yesterday.
B I ².................. (listen) to the new Green Day CD.
C I ³.................. (play) computer games.
D I ⁴.................. (surf) the Net all day.
E Where were you?! I ⁵.................. (wait) hours for you all!
                                              ☐ 5

5 **Look at the pictures and complete the sentences.**

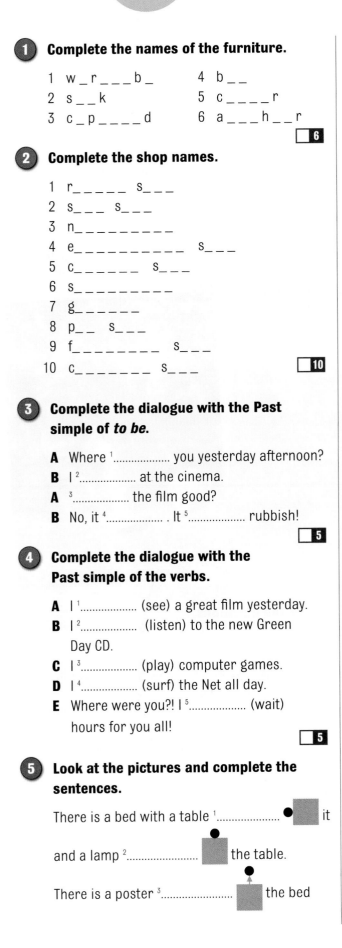

There is a bed with a table ¹.................. ● it

and a lamp ².................. the table.

There is a poster ³.................. the bed

and a rug ⁴.................. ● it. There is a guitar

⁵.................. ● ● the bed and the table

and a window ⁶.................. ● the bed.
                                              ☐ 6

6 **Write the questions.**

1 ....?
   I was a school at 4 pm.
2 ....?
   No, I wasn't in the kitchen. I was in the hall.
3 ....?
   No, the film wasn't very interesting!
4 ....?
   No, he wasn't happy.
5 ....?
   Yes, they were late!
                                              ☐ 10

7 **Complete the story with the Past simple tense of the verbs in brackets.**

Yesterday at 5 o'clock an accident ¹.................. (happen) in Forest Road. A woman ².................. (shout) for help. Mr Summers ³.................. (stop) his car. He ⁴.................. (jump) out of the car and ⁵.................. (phone) an ambulance. Ten minutes later an ambulance ⁶.................. (arrive). The paramedics ⁷.................. (help) the woman. Luckily she ⁸.................. (be) fine.
                                              ☐ 8

                                    TOTAL 50

My progress so far is ...

☺ **brilliant!**   ☐

😐 **quite good.**   ☐

☹ **not great.**   ☐

Free time activities

1 What are the five most popular free time activities for boys and girls in your country? Write a list of activities and decide with your class which are the most popular.

A What do you think is the most popular activity for boys?
B Football.
A How many people think football is the most popular activity?

39
2 Listen to the interview with Alison about her free time and circle the correct word.

1 In her free time Alison goes *skiing* / *swimming* .
2 She goes *once* / *twice* a week.
3 She's got a *competition* / *meeting* at the weekend.
4 She plays the *trumpet* / *guitar* .
5 Her mum doesn't like it because it's *boring* / *noisy* .

3 Read about this British hobby and answer the questions.

What's new in the playground?

Scoubidous are a fantastic new playground craze. They are pieces of coloured plastic string. You can make wristbands, key rings and ornaments for your bags and clothes. They're fun and they're cheap. They cost about 5p a string. I usually buy about 100 for £5. We all play with them at break time and lunchtime. Boys play with them too.

Fiona, 12, London

1 What are Scoubidous?
2 What can you make with them?
3 How much does a string cost?
4 How much do a hundred cost?
5 When do children play with them?

4 **Over 2 U!** What is a favourite hobby in your school? Write a paragraph.

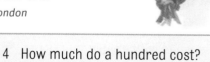 **MORE!** And now you can watch *Kids in the UK!*

Great Mysteries of the World:

Flight 19

Draw a line from Miami to the island of Bermuda in the Atlantic Ocean. Then draw another line from Bermuda to Puerto Rico in the Caribbean Sea. Finally go back from Puerto Rico to Miami. Inside the lines is a triangle: the famous Bermuda Triangle.

Over many years, a lot of ships and planes that went into the Bermuda Triangle did not come out again – they just disappeared. A famous incident was 'Flight 19' in 1945.

On 5th December, at 1.30 pm, five American Navy planes – 'Avengers' – left Florida and flew into the triangle. The pilots were experienced students. The weather was good. At about 3 pm, one of the pilots talked to the control tower: 'We're lost. Everything looks wrong.'

At 5 pm, the weather started to get bad. The pilots were still lost and they asked for help. At 7 pm in the evening, the control tower heard the pilots of the planes for the last time. No one ever saw the pilots or the planes again. The US Navy sent planes and ships to look for them, but they did not find anything to explain what happened to the planes.

Is this hard to believe? Well, here are some more days that planes disappeared in the Bermuda Triangle.

- February 22, 1978
- September 21, 1978
- February 11, 1980
- June 28, 1980
- January 6, 1981
- March 26, 1986
- October 31, 1991
- June 14, 1999

For **MORE!** Go to **www.cambridge.org/elt/more** and do a quiz on this text.

Wordlist

Starter section

apple /'æpl/
chicken /'tʃɪkɪn/
dictionary /'dɪkʃənri/
eight /eɪt/
eighteen /eɪ'tiːn/
eleven /ɪ'levən/
favourite /'feɪvərɪt/
fifteen /fɪf'tiːn/
fine /faɪn/
five /faɪv/
food /fuːd/
four /fɔː(r)/
fourteen /fɔː'tiːn/
friend /'frend/
friendly /'frendli/
from /frɒm/
fruit /fruːt/
good afternoon
    /gʊd ɑːftə'nuːn/
good evening /gʊd 'iːvnɪŋ/
good morning
    /gʊd 'mɔːnɪŋ/
good night /gʊd 'naɪt/
goodbye /gʊdbaɪ/
great /greɪt/
hamburger /'hæmbɜːgə(r)/
hamster /'hæmstə(r)/
hello /he'ləʊ/
her /hɜː(r)/
hi /haɪ/
his /hɪz/
horse /hɔːs/
house /haʊs/
ice cream /aɪs' kriːm/
late /leɪt/
nice /naɪs/
nine /naɪn/
nineteen /naɪn'tiːn/
number /'nʌmbə(r)/
one /wʌn/
pet /pet/
right /raɪt/
scared /skeəd/
seven /'sevən/
seventeen /sevən'tiːn/
six /sɪks/
sixteen /sɪk'stiːn/

sorry /'sɒri/
ten /ten/
thanks /θæŋks/
thirteen /θɜː'tiːn/
three /θriː/
twenty /'twenti/
twenty-one /twenti 'wʌn/
two /tuː/
where /weə(r)/
wrong /rɒŋ/

Unit 1

activity /æk'tɪvəti/
angry /'æŋgri/
another /ə'nʌðə(r)/
bad /bæd/
band /bænd/
beautiful /'bjuːtɪfəl/
bored /bɔːd/
boy /bɔɪ/
bus stop /'bʌs stɒp/
busy /'bɪzi/
bye /baɪ/
car /kɑː(r)/
city /'sɪti/
cold /kəʊld/
day /deɪ/
download /'daʊnləʊd/
duck /dʌk/
during /'djʊərɪŋ/
excited /ɪk'saɪtɪd/
fantastic /fæn'tæstɪk/
fast /fɑːst/
feel /fiːl/
football club /'fʊtbɔːl klʌb/
fun /fʌn/
happy /'hæpi/
here /hɪə(r)/
homework /'həʊmwɜːk/
hot /hɒt/
hungry /'hʌŋgri/
in front of /ɪn 'frʌnt əv/
meet /miːt/
museum /mjuː'ziːəm/
nervous /'nɜːvəs/
new /njuː/
one /wʌn/
sad /sæd/

school /skuːl/
select /sɪ'lekt/
shopping /'ʃɒpɪŋ/
sorry /'sɒri/
tired /'taɪəd/
tomorrow /tə'mɒrəʊ/
town /taʊn/
type /taɪp/
week /wiːk/
weekend /wiːk'end/

Unit 2

actor /'æktə(r)/
bag /bæg/
behind /bɪ'haɪnd/
board /bɔːd/
breakfast /'brekfəst/
capital /'kæpɪtəl/
castle /'kɑːsl/
cathedral /kə'θiːdrəl/
CD-player /ˌsiː 'diː ˌpleɪə(r)/
chair /tʃeə(r)/
to come /kʌm/
door /dɔːr/
empty /'empti/
film star /fɪlm stɑː(r)/
floor /flɔː(r)/
fly /flaɪ/
to hate /heɪt/
in /ɪn/
lake /leɪk/
to laugh /lɑːf/
to look /lʊk/
man / men /mæn, men/
Maths /mæθs/
messy /'mesi/
mother /'mʌðə(r)/
mountain /'maʊntɪn/
newspaper /'njuːspeɪpə(r)/
next to /nekst tuː, tə/
on /ɒn/
open /'əʊpən/
overhead projector
    /əʊvəhed prə'dʒektə(r)/
pencil case /'pensl keɪs/
person / people
    /pɜːsən, piːpl/
phone number
    /fəʊn nʌmbə(r)/

to pick up /pɪk 'ʌp/
pier /pɪə(r)/
pupil /'pjuːpəl/
quiet /kwaɪət/
right /raɪt/
river /'rɪvə(r)/
rugby /'rʌgbi/
sea /siː/
to sit /sɪt/
south /saʊθ/
sport /spɔːt/
stadium /'steɪdiəm/
to stand /stænd/
student /'stjuːdənt/
today /tə'deɪ/
tonight /tə'naɪt/
under /'ʌndə(r)/
watch /wɒtʃ/
why /waɪ/
window /'wɪndəʊ/

Unit 3

armchair /'ɑːmtʃeə(r)/
bath /bɑːθ/
bathroom /'bɑːθruːm/
bed /bed/
bedroom /'bedruːm/
big /bɪg/
bookshelf /'bʊkʃelf/
café /'kæfeɪ/
camel /'kæməl/
campsite /'kæmpsaɪt/
children /'tʃɪldrən/
cooker /'kʊkə(r)/
cupboard /'kʌbəd/
curtains /'kɜːtənz/
DVD player
    /diː viː diː pleɪə(r)/
early /'ɜːli/
eye /aɪ/
famous /'feɪməs/
forest /'fɒrɪst/
free /friː/
fridge /frɪdʒ/
garage /'gærɑːʒ/
hall /hɔːl/
hill /hɪl/
hippo /'hɪpəʊ/

ideal /aɪˈdiːəl/
kilometre /ˈkɪləmiːtə(r)/
kitchen /ˈkɪtʃɪn/
light /laɪt/
living room /ˈlɪvɪŋ ruːm/
monster /ˈmɒnstə(r)/
north-west /nɔːθ ˈwest/
owl /aʊl/
pelican /ˈpelɪkən/
place /pleɪs/
playground /ˈpleɪgraʊnd/
pony /ˈpəʊni/
pool /puːl/
poster /ˈpəʊstə(r)/
rabbit /ˈræbɪt/
ride /raɪd/
sandwich /ˈsændwɪtʃ/
screen /skriːn/
shelf /ʃelf/
shop /ʃɒp/
small /smɔːl/
sofa /ˈsəʊfə/
square /skweə(r)/
stereo /ˈsteriəʊ/
sure /ʃɔː/
swimming pool /ˈswɪmɪŋ puːl/
table /ˈteɪbl/
tell /tel/
toilet /ˈtɔɪlət/
torch /tɔːtʃ/
tree /triː/
trip /trɪp/
unfriendly /ʌnˈfrendli/
valley /ˈvæli/
wardrobe /ˈwɔːdrəʊb/
washbasin /ˈwɒʃbeɪsən/
watch /wɒtʃ/
zoo /zuː/

Unit 4

accent /ˈæksənt/
American /əˈmerɪkən/
arm /ɑːm/
art /ɑːt/
Austria /ˈɒstriə/
Austrian /ˈɒstriən/
banana /bəˈnɑːnə/
bear /beə(r)/
bicycle /ˈbaɪsɪkl/
biology /baɪˈɒlədʒi/
Brazil /brəˈzɪl/

Brazilian /brəˈzɪliən/
Britain /ˈbrɪtən/
British /ˈbrɪtɪʃ/
chemistry /ˈkemɪstri/
China /ˈtʃaɪnə/
Chinese /tʃaɪˈniːz/
comprehensive /kɒmprɪˈhensɪv/
cool /kuːl/
crocodile /ˈkrɒkədaɪl/
ear /ɪə(r)/
England /ˈɪŋglənd/
English /ˈɪŋglɪʃ/
fair /feə(r)/
feet /fiːt/
fingers /ˈfɪŋgəz/
Finland /ˈfɪnlənd/
Finnish /ˈfɪnɪʃ/
flag /flæg/
food /fuːd/
foot /fʊt/
France /frɑːns/
French /frentʃ/
frog /frɒg/
geography /dʒiˈɒgrəfi/
German /ˈdʒɜːmən/
Germany /ˈdʒɜːməni/
good-looking /gʊd ˈlʊkɪŋ/
gorilla /gəˈrɪlə/
Greece /griːs/
Greek /griːk/
hair /heə(r)/
hand /hænd/
head /hed/
History /ˈhɪstəri/
honey /ˈhʌni/
ice cream /aɪs ˈkriːm/
ICT /aɪ siː ˈtiː/
Ireland /ˈaɪələnd/
Irish /ˈaɪərɪʃ/
Italy /ˈɪtəli/
Japan /dʒəˈpæn/
Japanese /dʒæpəˈniːz/
jumper /ˈdʒʌmpə(r)/
left /left/
leg /leg/
long /lɒŋ/
look /lʊk/
money /ˈmʌni/
motorbike /ˈməʊtəbaɪk/
mouth /maʊθ/
Music /ˈmjuːzɪk/

news /njuːz/
nose /nəʊz/
PE /piː ˈiː/
penfriend /ˈpenfrend/
Physics /ˈfɪzɪks/
Poland /ˈpəʊlənd/
Polish /ˈpəʊlɪʃ/
RE /ɑːr ˈiː/
secondary /ˈsekəndri/
shirt /ʃɜːt/
short /ʃɔːt/
shoulder /ˈʃəʊldə(r)/
skateboard /ˈskeɪtbɔːd/
skirt /skɜːt/
Spain /speɪn/
Spanish /ˈspænɪʃ/
tall /tɔːl/
teeth /tiːθ/
toes /təʊz/
Turkey /ˈtɜːki/
Turkish /ˈtɜːkɪʃ/
umbrella /ʌmˈbrelə/
uniform /ˈjuːnɪfɔːm/
the USA /ðə juː es ˈeɪ/
wide-mouthed /ˈwaɪd maʊðd/

Unit 5

almost /ˈɔːlməʊst/
always /ˈɔːlweɪz/
barbecue /ˈbɑːbɪkjuː/
beef /biːf/
bread /bred/
bus /bʌs/
butter /ˈbʌtə(r)/
buy /baɪ/
cabbage /ˈkæbɪdʒ/
carrot /ˈkærət/
carry /ˈkæri/
cheese /tʃiːz/
cherries /ˈtʃeriz/
chicken /ˈtʃɪkɪn/
chips /tʃɪps/
clothes /kləʊðz/
coffee /ˈkɒfi/
corner /ˈkɔːnə(r)/
curry /ˈkʌri/
dear /dɪə(r)/
dinner /ˈdɪnə(r)/
to do /duː/
drink /drɪŋk/
eggs /egz/

every /ˈevri/
father /ˈfɑːðə(r)/
fish /fɪʃ/
fishing /ˈfɪʃɪŋ/
fruit /fruːt/
grapes /greɪps/
hamburger /ˈhæmbɜːgə(r)/
to hate /heɪt/
hot dog /ˈhɒt dɒg/
hurry /ˈhʌri/
junk food /ˈdʒʌŋk fuːd/
to kiss /kɪs/
kiwi /ˈkiːwiː/
lunch /lʌntʃ/
mango /ˈmæŋgəʊ/
meat /miːt/
milk /mɪlk/
to miss /mɪs/
month /mʌnθ/
never /ˈnevə(r)/
noodles /ˈnuːdlz/
of course /əv ˈkɔːs/
often /ˈɒftən, ˈɒfn/
once /wʌns/
onion /ˈʌnjən/
orange /ˈɒrɪndʒ/
orange juice /ˈɒrɪndʒ dʒuːs/
pork /pɔːk/
potato /pəˈteɪtəʊ/
to relax /rɪˈlæks/
restaurant /ˈrestrɒnt/
rice /raɪs/
sausage /ˈsɒsɪdʒ/
sometimes /ˈsʌmtaɪmz/
soup /suːp/
spinach /ˈspɪnɪtʃ/
steak /steɪk/
strawberry /ˈstrɔːbri/
sweets /swiːts/
to take /teɪk/
tea /tiː/
tidy /ˈtaɪdi/
tomato /təˈmɑːtəʊ/
true /truː/
usually /ˈjuːʒuəli/
vegetable /ˈvedʒtəbl/
to wash /wɒʃ/
weird /wɪəd/
work /wɜːk/

Unit 6

answer /ˈɑːnsə(r)/
away /əˈweɪ/
baby /ˈbeɪbi/
before /bɪˈfɔː(r)/
to begin /bɪˈgɪn/
boring /ˈbɔːrɪŋ/
brother /ˈbrʌðə(r)/
to clean /kliːn/
clock /klɒk/
to cook /kʊk/
crisps /krɪsps/
to cut /kʌt/
end /end/
family /ˈfæməli/
farm /fɑːm/
to feed /fiːd/
film /fɪlm/
friend /frend/
to get up /get ˈʌp/
to go /gəʊ/
grass /grɑːs/
guitar /gɪˈtɑː(r)/
gym /dʒɪm/
to hang out /hæŋ ˈaʊt/
to have breakfast
    /hæv ˈbrekfəst/
to hold on /həʊld ˈɒn/
to hope /həʊp/
hour /ˈaʊə(r)/
interesting /ˈɪntərəstɪŋ/
joke /dʒəʊk/
to knock /nɒk/
to know /nəʊ/
to leave /liːv/
life /laɪf/
to listen to /ˈlɪsən tuː, tə/
to live /lɪv/
o'clock /əˈklɒk/
parents /ˈpeərənts/
phone /fəʊn/
piano /piˈænəʊ/
to play /pleɪ/
problem /ˈprɒbləm/
programme /ˈprəʊgræm/
to read /riːd/
rhyme /raɪm/
to ride a horse
    /ˌraɪd ə ˈhɔːs/
rock /rɒk/
roller skating
    /ˈrəʊlə ˌskeɪtɪŋ/

romantic /rəʊˈmæntɪk/
same /seɪm/
slap /slæp/
to speak /spiːk/
to start /stɑːt/
to surf /sɜːf/
to talk /tɔːk/
thing /θɪŋ/
to understand /ˌʌndəˈstænd/
village /ˈvɪlɪdʒ/
to visit /ˈvɪzɪt/
to walk /wɔːk/
to want /wɒnt/
water buffalo
    /ˈwɔːtə ˌbʌfələʊ/
to write /raɪt/

Unit 7

a lot /ə ˈlɒt/
alright /ɔːlˈraɪt/
to arrive /əˈraɪv/
basketball /ˈbɑːskɪtbɔːl/
beans /biːnz/
birthday /ˈbɜːθdeɪ/
box /bɒks/
cap /kæp/
to carry /ˈkæri/
changing room
    /ˈtʃeɪndʒɪŋ ruːm/
to come back /kʌm ˈbæk/
cycling /ˈsaɪklɪŋ/
drawer /ˈdrɔː/
dress /dres/
excuse me /ɪkˈskjuːz miː/
expensive /ɪkˈspensɪv/
gallop /ˈgæləp/
to give /gɪv/
granny /ˈgræni/
to hear /hɪə(r)/
hole /həʊl/
how much /haʊ mʌtʃ/
jacket /ˈdʒækɪt/
jeans /dʒiːnz/
key-ring /ˈkiː rɪŋ/
to lend /lend/
lucky /ˈlʌki/
mobile phone
    /ˌməʊbaɪl ˈfəʊn/
outside /aʊtˈsaɪd/
over there /ˌəʊvə ˈðeə(r)/
pair /peə(r)/
parrot /ˈpærət/

party /ˈpɑːti/
price /praɪs/
rich /rɪtʃ/
to run /rʌn/
to see /siː/
shoe /ʃuː/
sock /sɒk/
sugar /ˈʃʊgə(r)/
sweater /ˈswetə(r)/
top /tɒp/
trainers /ˈtreɪnərz/
trousers /ˈtraʊzəz/
to try on /ˌtraɪ ˈɒn/
T-shirt /ˈtiː ʃɜːt/
volleyball /ˈvɒlibɔːl/
to wear /weə(r)/
winter /ˈwɪntə(r)/
woods /wʊdz/
to worry /ˈwʌri/

Unit 8

already /ɔːlˈredi/
aunt /ɑːnt/
to borrow /ˈbɒrəʊ/
cereal /ˈsɪəriəl/
to check out /tʃek ˈaʊt/
classical /ˈklæsɪkəl/
to climb /klaɪm/
cousin /ˈkʌzən/
to dance /dɑːns/
darling /ˈdɑːlɪŋ/
difficult /ˈdɪfɪkəlt/
drums /drʌmz/
face /feɪs/
fine /faɪn/
fit /fɪt/
fried /fraɪd/
golf /gɒlf/
grandfather /ˈgrænfɑːðə(r)/
grandmother
    /ˈgrænmʌðə(r)/
grandparents
    /ˈgrænpeərənts/
heaven /ˈhevn/
instrument /ˈɪnstrəmənt/
to juggle /ˈdʒʌgl/
keyboards /ˈkiːbɔːdz/
language /ˈlæŋgwɪdʒ/
musical /ˈmjuːzɪkl/
opposite /ˈɒpəzɪt/
perfect /ˈpɜːfɪkt/
pet /pet/

photo album
    /ˈfəʊtəʊ ˌælbəm/
popular /ˈpɒpjələ(r)/
to practise /ˈpræktɪs/
to rollerblade /ˈrəʊləbleɪd/
secret /ˈsiːkrət/
to show /ʃəʊ/
to sing /sɪŋ/
slice /slaɪs/
to smile /smaɪl/
stick /stɪk/
tongue /tʌŋ/
to touch /tʌtʃ/
trick /trɪk/
uncle /ˈʌŋkl/
to water-ski /ˈwɔːtə skiː/
way /weɪ/
western /ˈwestən/
wiggle /ˈwɪgl/
to work out /wɜːk ˈaʊt/

Unit 9

air /eə(r)/
April /ˈeɪprəl/
August /ˈɔːgəst/
bookshop /ˈbʊkʃɒp/
candle /ˈkændl/
to celebrate /ˈselibreɪt/
clue /kluː/
colouring /ˈkʌlərɪŋ/
December /dɪˈsembə(r)/
to disturb /dɪˈstɜːb/
to enjoy /ɪnˈdʒɔɪ/
envelope /ˈenvələʊp/
exact /ɪgˈzækt/
February /ˈfebruəri/
finally /ˈfaɪnəli/
first /fɜːst/
forehead /ˈfɔːhed/
holiday /ˈhɒlədeɪ/
January /ˈdʒænjuəri/
July /dʒʊˈlaɪ/
June /dʒuːn/
to lift /lɪft/
luck /lʌk/
March /mɑːtʃ/
May /meɪ/
moment /ˈməʊmənt/
November /nəʊˈvembə(r)/
October /ɒkˈtəʊbə(r)/
present /ˈprezənt/
to rain /reɪn/

to raise /reɪz/
ready /'redi/
roller skate /'rəʊlə skeɪt/
sauce /sɔːs/
second /'sekənd/
to send /send/
September /sep'tembə(r)/
soon /suːn/
special /'speʃəl/
to swim /swɪm/
table tennis /'teɪbl ˌtenɪs/
text message /'tekst ˌmesɪʤ/
warm /wɔːm/
to win /wɪn/
year /jɪə(r)/

Unit 10

airport /'eəpɔːt/
average /'ævərɪʤ/
to back up /bæk 'ʌp/
balloon /bə'luːn/
to burn /bɜːn/
cage /keɪʤ/
to check /tʃek/
chore /tʃɔː(r)/
to collect /kə'lekt/
to decorate /'dekəreɪt/
doctor /'dɒktə(r)/
to fix /fɪks/
free time /'friː taɪm/
garden gnome /ˌgɑːdn 'nəʊm/
guide /gaɪd/
hard disk /hɑːd 'dɪsk/
hospital /'hɒspɪtəl/
household /'haʊshəʊld/
invitation /ɪnvɪ'teɪʃən/
lantern /'læntən/
part-time /pɑːt 'taɪm/
pocket money /'pɒkɪt ˌmʌni/
policeman /pə'liːsmən/
program /'prəʊgræm/
ringtone /'rɪŋtəʊn/
shower /'ʃaʊə(r)/
to sleep /sliːp/
to spend /spend/
sunglasses /'sʌnglɑːsɪz/
trendy /'trendi/
virus /'vaɪrəs/
wrong /rɒŋ/

Unit 11

basket /'bɑːskɪt/
bedside table /ˌbedsaɪd 'teɪbl/
to believe /bɪ'liːv/
butler /'bʌtlə(r)/
carpet /'kɑːpɪt/
cinema /'sɪnəmə/
congratulations /kəngrætʃə'leɪʃnz/
cook /kʊk/
diamonds /'daɪəməndz/
diary /'daɪəri/
flowers /'flaʊə(r)z/
lamp /læmp/
library /'laɪbrəri/
maid /meɪd/
missing /'mɪsɪŋ/
plate /pleɪt/
to prepare /prɪ'peə(r)/
robber /'rɒbə(r)/
robbery /'rɒbəri/
rug /rʌg/
shopping centre /'ʃɒpɪŋ ˌsentə(r)/
sink /sɪŋk/
valuable /'væljubl/
yesterday /'jestədeɪ/

Unit 12

accident /'æksɪdənt/
ago /ə'gəʊ/
ambulance /'æmbjələnts/
to chase /tʃeɪs/
to clean /kliːn/
director /də'rektə(r), dɪ-, daɪ-/
DVD-drive /ˌdiː viː 'diː draɪv/
electronics /elek'trɒnɪks/
end of the world /ˌend əv ðə 'wɜːld/
to finish /'fɪnɪʃ/
flatscreen /'flætskriːn/
furniture /'fɜːnɪtʃə(r)/
goal /gəʊl/
grocer's /'grəʊsəz/
to happen /'hæpən/
horror /'hɒrə(r)/
to interview /'ɪntəvjuː/
to jump /ʤʌmp/
newsagent's /'njuːzeɪʤənts/

to notice /'nəʊtɪs/
to phone /fəʊn/
police /pə'liːs/
to push /pʊʃ/
to relax /rɪ'læks/
to rescue /'reskjuː/
rose /rəʊz/
rubbish /'rʌbɪʃ/
score /skɔː(r)/
sculpture /'skʌlptʃə(r)/
to shout /ʃaʊt/
to spill /spɪl/
to store /stɔː(r)/
sunny /'sʌni/
team /tiːm/
trumpet /'trʌmpɪt/

Pronunciation guide

Vowels

/iː/	see
/ɪ/	bit
/e/	bed
/æ/	sad
/ɑː/	father
/ʌ/	cut
/ʊ/	cook
/uː/	too
/i/	happy
/ə/	above
/ɒ/	got
/ɔː/	saw
/u/	actual

Diphthongs

/ɜː/	circle
/eɪ/	say
/aɪ/	buy
/ɔɪ/	boy
/əʊ/	go
/aʊ/	now
/ɪə/	hear
/eə/	hair
/ʊə/	sure
/juː/	few
/aɪə/	fire
/aʊə/	power

Consonants

/p/	push
/b/	bank
/t/	time
/d/	diary
/k/	carpet
/g/	big
/f/	surf
/v/	very
/θ/	thin
/ð/	that
/s/	sit
/z/	zero
/ʃ/	shine
/ʒ/	measure
/h/	hot
/w/	water
/tʃ/	chair
/dʒ/	joke
/m/	more
/n/	snow
/ŋ/	sing
/r/	ring
/l/	small
/j/	you

CAMBRIDGE UNIVERSITY PRESS
www.cambridge.org/elt

HELBLING LANGUAGES
www.helblinglanguages.com

More! 1 Student's Book
by Herbert Puchta & Jeff Stranks
with G. Gerngross C. Holzmann P. Lewis-Jones

© Cambridge University Press and Helbling Languages 2008
(*More* was originally published by Helbling Languages © Helbling Languages 2006)

First published 2008
4th printing 2009

Printed   in the United Kingdom at the University Press, Cambridge

A catalogue record for this publication is available from the British Library

ISBN   978-0-521-71293-4   More! 1 Student's Book with interactive CD-ROM (Windows)
ISBN   978-0-521-71294-1   More! 1 Workbook with CD (audio)
ISBN   978-0-521-71295-8   More! 1 Teacher's Book
ISBN   978-0-521-71296-5   More! 1 Teacher's Resource Pack with Testbuilder CD-ROM (Windows) / CD (audio)
ISBN   978-0-521-71297-2   More! 1 Class CDs (audio)
ISBN   978-0-521-71298-9   More! 1 Extra Practice Book
ISBN   978-0-521-71299-6   More! 1 DVD (PAL/NTSC)

The authors would like to thank those people who have made significant contributions towards the final form of MORE! INTERNATIONAL:

Oonagh Wade and Rosamund Cantalamessa for their expertise in working on the manuscripts, their useful suggestions for improvement, and the support we got from them.

Lucia Astuti and Markus Spielmann, Helbling Languages, Ron Ragsdale and James Dingle, Cambridge University Press, for their dedication to the project and innovative publishing vision.

Our designers, Amanda Hockin, Greg Sweetnam, Quantico, Craig Cornell and Niels Gyde for their imaginative layouts and stimulating creativity. Also, our artwork assistants, Silvia Scorzoso and Francesca Gironi, for their dedicated work.

The publishers would like to thank the following for their kind permission to reproduce the following photographs and other copyright material:

Alamy p7, p9 (Mike, Jane, Simon, Jackie, Erica), p11, p18, p21, p28 (Google interface), p29, p32, p38, p45, p46, p49 (brown bats), p55 (Sara), p56 (Alex), p58, p65 (CD: Food Icons; students in class), p66 (Sanjit), p68, p69, p72, p75, p78 (girl), p82, p85, p92, p98, p101, p106, p108, p109 (cuckoo; aquarium), p111, p115, p116, p118, p124, p127, p128 (Turkish lira; Swedish money), p129 (New York City 1894), p138; **Boehmer Family** p95; **Dr. Eric H. Chudler, Neuroscience for Kids** (http://faculty.washington.edu/chudler/neurok.html) p48; **CNG coins** (http://www.cngcoins.com) p128 (the Lydian coin); **Corbis** p9 (Tom), p18 (Rebecca), p45 (Pets' corner), p55 (Madeleine), p65 (vegetables), p78 (boy), p92 (grandmother; grandfather), p129 (Mint Workers; IBM Computer); **Günter Gerngross** p49 (sleeping lions); **Helbling Languages** p14 (pizza; football; hamburger; chair), p99; ©iStockphoto.com/ericsphotography p7 (two boys talking), /lubilub /hartcreations p12, /DNY59 /texasmary /sjlocke /matthewleesdixon /arsenik /groveb /dlHunter /gynane /dalton00 /CampSpot /RainforestAustralia /marmion p14, /Ravet007 / Sportstock p15, /nano /scottdunlap p28, /LizV /dndavis p34, / fstop123 /JacquesKloppers /ROMAOSLO p45 (café; playground; girl riding pony), /Gelpi /tudorish p49 (dolphins; giraffe), /ivar p55 (Sylvie), /aabejon /imagepointphoto /Malven /hartcreations / LynnSeeden /LUGO p56, /barsik /dishapaun p64, /ronen /woodstock p66, /marcel63 p88, /nojustice /imagepointphoto p94, /SteveStone /Thomas_EyeDesign /Kuzma p105, /biffspandex /thejack /magui80 p109, /agmit p128 (pounds), /ManoAfrica /anthony_taylor p129 (shell; bank card); **The Naval Historical Center** p139; **Herbert Puchta** p49 (leopard); **Gian J. Quasar** p139 (map of Bermuda Triangle).

The publishers would like to thank the following illustrators:

Roberto Battestini; Barbara Bonci; Moreno Chiacchiera; Giovanni Da Re; Pietro Dichiara; Michele Farella; Sergio Giantomassi; Pierluigi Longo; Piet Luthi; Asia Nicitto; Giovanni Rolandi; Francesca Scarponi; Lucilla Stellato.

The publishers would like to thank the following for their assistance with commissioned photographs:

David Tolley Ltd. pp 20, 21, 30, 40, 50, 60, 70, 80, 85, 90, 100, 110, 120 (diary), 130; Studio Antonietti pp 36, 106 (red envelope).

Every effort has been made to trace the owners of any copyright material in this book. If notified, the publisher will be pleased to rectify any errors or omissions.